THE
SOCCER GAMES
BOOK

To Kenny and John
To the game they play
and
To Joseph Simon
Who believed that the sun
never set on soccer

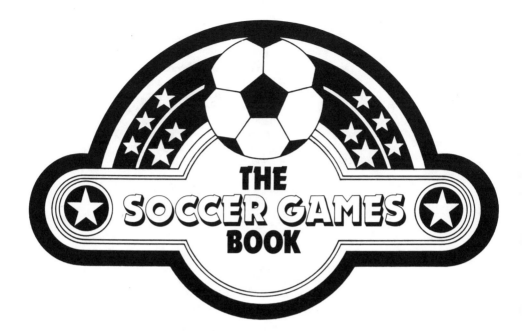

by
J. Malcolm Simon
New Jersey Institute of Technology
and
John A. Reeves
University of Rochester

LEISURE PRESS
Champaign, Illinois

Library of Congress Catalog Card Number:
82-81817
ISBN 0-88011-064-3

10   9

Front cover photo by Wayne Glusker
Back cover photo by Tom Salvas
Book and cover design by Diana J. Goodin
Typeset by turnaround, Berkeley

PHOTO CREDITS
Bill Clare: page 5
Phil Degginger: page 6
Tom Salvas: page 16, 58, 116
Joe Van Woerden: page 8

Leisure Press
A Division of Human Kinetics
Web site: http:⁄⁄www.humankinetics.com/

United States:
Human Kinetics, P.O. Box 5076, Champaign, IL 61825-5076
1-800-747-4457
e-mail: humank@hkusa.com

Canada:
Human Kinetics, Box 24040, Windsor, ON N8Y 4Y9
1-800-465-7301 (in Canada only)
e-mail: humank@hkcanada.com

Europe:
Human Kinetics, P.O. Box IW14, Leeds LS16 6TR, United Kingdom
(44) 1132 781708
e-mail: humank@hkeurope.com

Australia:
Human Kinetics, 57A Price Avenue, Lower Mitcham, South Australia 5062
(08) 277 1555
e-mail: humank@hkaustralia.com

New Zealand:
Human Kinetics, P.O. Box 105-231, Auckland 1
(09) 523 3462
e-mail: humank@hknewz.com

CONTENTS

PREFACE

To scrimmage or not to scrimmage: That is the question. This is a dilemma faced by novice and experienced coach alike. How much and when to scrimmage and/or drill is a real concern to the "parent-coach" facing a group of eager boys and girls who want to "play" and to the experienced high school or college coach who, despite all his planning, realizes his players are just going through the motions of drilling without any significant learning taking place.

The importance of drills cannot be overemphasized. The authors' appreciation of this importance is illustrated in our book, *The Coaches Collection of Soccer Drills*. Constant drilling, however, can be boring and ineffective, as can an inordinate reliance on scrimmaging. There is, however, a viable alternative to drilling and scrimmaging and this is the use of soccer related games.

Soccer related games are useful in coaching soccer. Games, which emphasize soccer techniques and tactics, can add variety to practice sessions keeping them interesting, enjoyable and productive. While useful for all ages, games are particularly helpful in coaching the young player who has a short attention span. Regardless of the players' ages and levels of ability, interest is kept high and the response to skill learning is better in an atmosphere of competition and fun.

To be effective, games should meet certain objectives:
- They should have some purpose or emphasis.
- They should allow for repetition or action, particularly in the technique or tactic being emphasized.
- They should call for some measure of control or accuracy.
- They should simulate game conditions.
- They should be fun.

The games included in this book are designed to meet these objectives. Most of them have been collected or created by the authors during their combined forty-four years as college soccer coaches. Other games included have been submitted by some of the most successful high school and college coaches in the United States. The reader can use all of these games or the ones that best fit his needs.

All information necessary for the effective organization of each game is included in its heading. Directly below the title, from left to right, are the emphases (primary emphasis capitalized), and the recommended playing area, number of players, and type of equipment.

The games are indexed in four different ways; (1) alphabetically by title, (2) according to the primary emphasis, (3) according to either primary or secondary emphasis, and (4) by the names of the contributing coach if other than the authors.

The authors are grateful to those coaches who contributed to this collection of games. We also express our deep appreciation to Mary Monaco for her diligent preparation of this manuscript.

J. Malcolm Simon and John A. Reeves

INDEX OF GAMES

GAME	GAME NUMBER

GAME	GAME NUMBER

GAME	GAME NUMBER

INDEX OF PRIMARY EMPHASES

INDEX OF PRIMARY AND SECONDARY EMPHASES

EMPHASIS	GAME NUMBER
Shielding	70,71,98
Shooting	1,2,5,8,15,19,37,38,46,50,73,74,86, 87,95,101,102,103,107,108,109,110, 111,112,126,130,131,136,144,146, 150,152,155,160
Support	55,154
Tackling	26,28,115,132
Throwing	12,104,142

INDEX OF CONTRIBUTING AUTHORS

CONTRIBUTOR	INSTITUTION	GAME NUMBER
Albert, Al	College of William and Mary	15
Bacon, Fran	University of Bridgeport	106
Boles, John	Temple University	98
Broadbent, Ronald	SUNY at Brockport	65
Chyzowych, Eugene	Columbia High School	47
Coulthart, Bill	Jacksonville University	42
Coven, Michael	Brandeis University	83
Crandall, Robert	Elmira College	157
Daoust, Richard	John F. Kennedy High School	109
DePeppe, William	Freehold Township High School	58
Dikranian, Armand	Southern Connecticut State College	100
Egli, James	Slippery Rock State College	138
Fellenbaum, John	Franklin and Marshall College	119
Goldman, Howard	Marist College	152
Goodyear, Alan	Rensselaer Polytechnic Institute	85
Griffith, Tom	Dartmouth College	75, 150
Gross, Larry M.	North Carolina State University	116
Harris, Dan	University of Wisconsin-Milwaukee	36
Henni, Geza	University of Rhode Island	5
Howell, Gordie	Rollins College	20
Hyndman, Schellas	Eastern Illinois University	21
Ibrahim, I.M.	Clemson University	30
Kline, Loren	University of Delaware	4, 148
Kullen, Robert A.	University of New Hampshire	23
Kutler, Kenneth	Frostburg State College	107
Lewis, Bud	Wilmington College	39, 96
Logan, George	San Diego State University	7, 105
Long, Leonard	Virginia Wesleyan College	113
Lyle, Donald L.	Grove City College	82
Makuvek, John	Moravian College	41
Martin, Jay	Ohio Wesleyan University	18, 77

CONTRIBUTOR	INSTITUTION	GAME NUMBER
Martin, Thomas R.	West Virginia Wesleyan College	81
Matlack, Charles	Earlham College	80
McEachen, Ron	Middlebury College	44
McMullan, John F.	Oceanside High School	102
McStay, Ron	Neptune High School	108
Miller, Jay	Tampa University	12
Muse, William	Princeton University	127
Myers, Will	William Paterson College	25
Mykulak, Nick	Stevens Institute of Technology	55
Nye, Robert E.	The College of Wooster	34
Olmer, Richard	Southhold High School	11
Parsons, Gary	Oakland University	76, 160
Rennie, John	Duke University	17
Rikstad, Art	North Plainfield High School	93
Rogers, C. William	Babson College	46
Sagastume, Luis	United States Air Force Academy	9
Scarborough, Don A.	Brevard College	79
Schmalz, Fred	University of Evansville	136
Seal, William A. III	McDonogh School	71
Seddon, Robert	University of Pennsylvania	10
Shellenberger, Bill	Lynchburg College	63
Shewcraft, Ronald W.	North Adams State College	141
Smith, Stephen	Fairport Central Schools	158
Stromecky, Ostap	University of Alabama-Huntsville	131
Taylor, Tom	West Essex High School	24
Tyson, Chris	SUNY at Stony Brook	143
Unger, Ernie	Paramus High School	40
Whitehouse, Marc	Gordon College	59
Wright, Owen	Elizabethtown College	99
Zelz, Lawrence J.	Gettysburg College	50

GAMES 1-160

1

ACCURACY KICK

| SHOOTING | 30 yd. Area in Front of Goal | 2 or more Players | 10 Balls |

Passing

Formation: Players stand thirty yards in front of a goal.

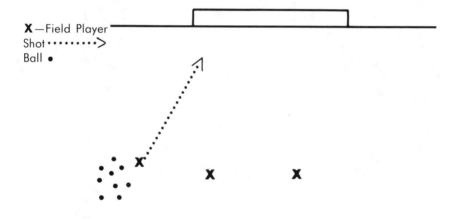

X—Field Player
Shot ·········>
Ball •

Procedure: Each player kicks a stationary ball at goal from a distance of thirty yards. Each player has ten attempts to accumulate a score. Five points are awarded for a ball that enters the goal on the fly, three points for a ball entering on one bounce and two points for a ball entering on two or more bounces. The player with the highest score after all players have completed the activity wins.

2

ACCURACY SHOOTING

SHOOTING	20 yd. Area in Front of Kickboard	2 or more Players	1 Ball per Player
			Kickboard

Formation: Two players, each with a ball, stand about twenty yards from a kickboard. A regulation goal is marked on the board. A dotted line is marked parallel to and one foot from each upright.

X—Field Player

Shot ·······>

Ball •

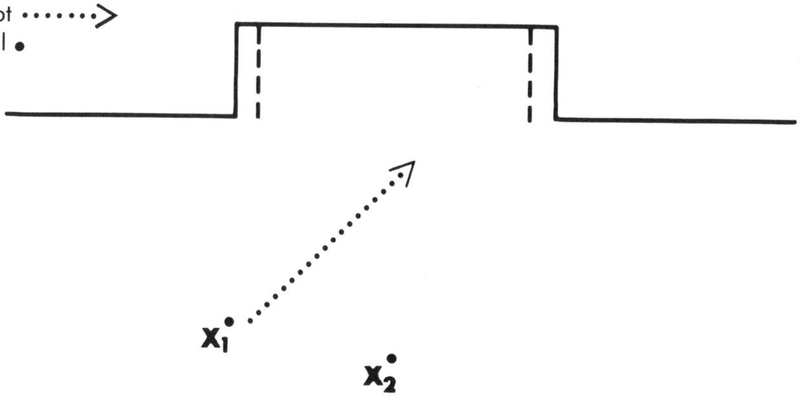

Procedure: Players alternate in taking ten free shots on the goal marked on the kickboard. Three points are scored for each shot landing within the marked one-foot area.

Variation:
• Take left- or right-footed shots only.
• Take shots closer to or further from a goal.

3

AIR SOCCER

CONTROL	20 yd. by 20 yd. Area	8 Players	1 Ball
Heading			2 Small Goals
Kicking			

Formation: Two teams of four players each are spread out in the area. One player has a ball. There are two indoor size goals.

X—Field Player
Ball •

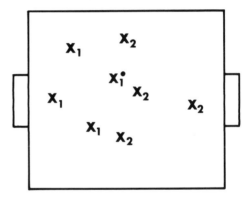

Procedure: This is a four vs. four game with the ball always played in the air. Ball possession is lost to the opponent when the ball touches the ground. Tackling is not allowed, only interceptions. Shots may be taken from anywhere. The team ahead after a set time period, or the first team to score a set number of goals, wins.

4

ALL OR NOTHING BASEBALL

RECEIVING   ½ Field   10 to 40 Players   1 Ball
Passing   3 Cones
Kicking

Contributor: *Loren Kline, University of Delaware, Newark, Delaware 19711*

Formation: There are two teams of equal numbers. The team "at bat" is the offensive team and forms a line on the goal line outside the goal. The defensive team spreads out in half field. One defensive player, with a soccer ball, is on the penalty mark. Three cones are used as bases.

D—Defensive Player
O—Offensive Player
Pass ------>
Sprint ----->>
Ball •
Cone ⊙

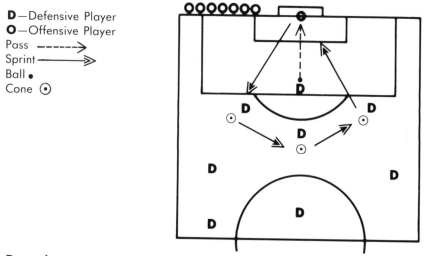

Procedure: The player with the ball kicks a rolling ball from the penalty mark to the goal line. The offensive player "at bat" kicks the ball into the field and attempts to touch all the bases and reach home (the goal line between the goals) before the players in the field get the ball into the goal. The field players must use soccer skills to get the ball home. Each play is a goal or an out and each player has a turn "at bat" before the teams change. The game can be played for any number of innings.

5

ATTACKING SOCCER

SHOOTING	½ Field	8 to 24 Players	3 Balls
			8 Cones
Heading		2 Goalkeepers	2 Portable Goals
Offensive and Defensive Techniques			

Contributor: *Geza Henni, University of Rhode Island, Kingston, Rhode Island 02881*

Formation: Four players (X1) play against four others (X2) in half field. Each team has a goalkeeper. Regulation goals are used. Cones are used to mark the corners and the penalty area at mid-field.

G—Goalkeeper
X—Field Player
Ball •
Cone ⊙

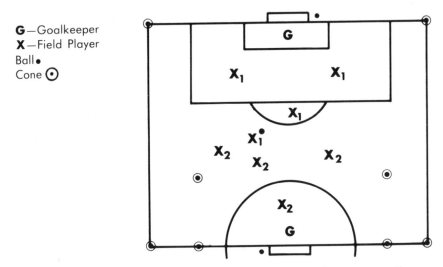

Procedure: The two teams play a half-field game for five minutes. Players cannot be offsides. Each player is assigned a specific opponent to mark. Goals are scored by heading or from shots taken outside the eighteen yard line. Goals scored from outside the eighteen yard line count two points, while goals scored by heading inside the eighteen count one point. To observe a ratio between work and rest, teams play for five minutes and rest for ten minutes while two other games are being played. Each team plays three games.

6

ATTACK vs DEFENSE

OFFENSIVE AND DEFENSIVE TECHNIQUES	½ Field	10 Players	1 Ball
		Goalkeeper	

Formation: Five attackers, one with a ball, and five defenders are in one half of the soccer field. A goalkeeper is in goal.

D—Defensive Player
G—Goalkeeper
O—Offensive Player
Ball •

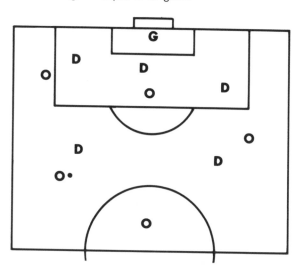

Procedure: Five attackers play against five defenders and a goalkeeper for ten minutes. The attackers try to score, while the defenders try to get the ball across midfield when they gain possession.
    The attackers score five points for a goal, two points for a corner kick and one point for an offensive throw in. The defenders score one point each time they interpass the ball across mid-field, after which the attackers restart play from mid-field.
    The goalkeeper may only throw the ball. A goal kick is taken by the goalie throwing the ball from the goal area. After ten minutes, the teams change roles and play continues for ten more minutes. The team scoring the most points wins.

7

AZTEC SPECIAL

OFFENSIVE AND DEFENSIVE TECHNIQUES	20 yd. by 20 yd. Area	5 to 9 Players	1 Ball
			8 Cones

Contributor: *George R. Logan, San Diego State University, San Diego, California 92182*

Formation: Four goals, numbered 1-4, border the area. Each goal is one yard wide, marked by two cones. One player stands by each goal, and a fifth player is juggling the ball in the center of the arena.

X—Field Player
Ball •
Cone ⊙

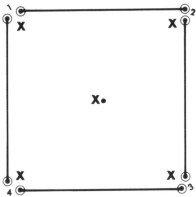

Procedure: The coach calls out the numbers of two goals; e.g. "3 and 1." The players by these goals become the defenders and guard the first numbered goal (3). The remaining two players join with the center player in attacking the specified goal only. Should the defenders gain possession, they can attack any of the other three goals. If the ball goes out of bounds, it is put back in play by a free pass. Keep playing until a goal is scored or for a specified time period.

Variation:
- Double up on players; i.e., use pairs at goal.
- Widen the goals.
- Increase the size of playing area.
- Take away a goal possibility from the defenders; e.g., the second number called cannot be scored on.

8

BACK PASS SHOT

SHOOTING   ½ Field   10 or more Players 1 Ball

                                        Goalkeeper

Offensive and Defensive
Techniques

Formation: One team of five players is on attack against five defenders in half field. The goalkeeper is in goal.

D—Defensive Player
G—Goalkeeper
O—Offensive Player
Pass ─ ─ ─ ─ ─>
Shot • • • • • • • • >
Ball •

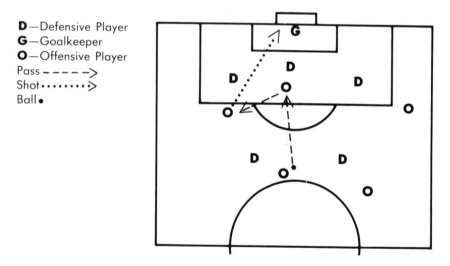

Procedure: Play begins with a kickoff and continues as in regulation soccer. However, shots on goal may only be taken after a back pass from an attacker who has penetrated the penalty area.

9

BALL TAG

PASSING	½ Field	11 Players	10 Balls

Fitness

Contributor: *Luis Sagastume, United States Air Force Academy, Colorado Springs, Colorado 80840*

Formation: Ten players line up along one sideline. One player, with a supply of balls, stands in the middle of the area.

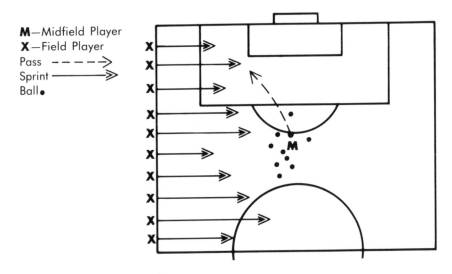

M—Midfield Player
X—Field Player
Pass ‒ ‒ ‒ ‒ ‒ >
Sprint ————>
Ball •

Procedure: On a signal, the players on the sideline try to sprint to the opposite side of the field without being hit below the waist by a ball passed or shot by the midfield player. Once a player is hit, he joins the middle player in trying to hit the runners. Only inside of the foot passes or shots may be used to hit runners. Keep playing until one player is left.

10

BASEBALL SOCCER

KICKING	Corner Area of Field	18 Players	1 Ball
Passing			4 Bases

Contributor: *Robert Seddon, University of Pennsylvania, Philadelphia, Pennsylvania 19104*

Formation: One corner area of a soccer field is set up like a baseball diamond including home plate and three bases. Nine players are on the team at bat and nine players are in the field. One player is in the pitching area with a soccer ball.

P—Pitcher
X—Field Player
Pass — — — →
Ball •

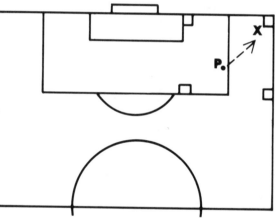

Procedure: The pitcher passes a rolling ball on the ground to the player at bat. The game is played like regulation baseball but with the following exceptions:
- Any air ball hit into the outfield and trapped in flight or after one bounce is an out.
- A foul ball is an out.
- There is no bunting, leading off bases or stealing.
- Ground balls must be controlled with the feet and passed to the appropriate base.
- The team at bat can have three or six outs.

All other baseball rules apply, such as forceouts, etc. The game can last seven or nine innings.

11 – BASSOC BALL

OFFENSIVE AND DEFENSIVE TECHNIQUES	Basketball Court	12 to 30 Players	1 Ball
			4 Cones

Contributor: *Richard Olmer, Southhold High School, Southhold, New York 11971*

Formation: Three offensive and three defensive players are positioned on a basketball court. Groups of three offensive and three defensive players are lined up on the side lines of the court. Three goal-keepers protect the two soccer goals marked by cones, at the end of the court.

X—Field Player
Ball •
Cone ⊙

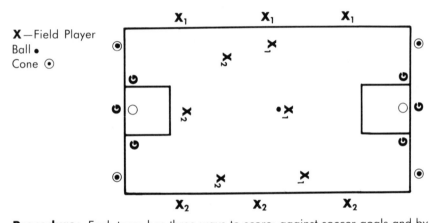

Procedure: Each team has three ways to score; against soccer goals and by scoring a basketball goal. Goalkeepers attempt to stop shots on goal; however, only defensive players may stop shots at the basketball goal. Balls lower than waist level are played by offensive and defensive players by using soccer skills. When the ball is above waist level, basketball skills are used. The exceptions are that players may dribble basketball style or drop the ball from hands to resume soccer skills. When a goalkeeper stops a shot, he throws the ball to players on his team on the sideline who throw the ball back into play. After a designated period of time, goalkeepers become field players, field players become sideline players, and sideline players become goalkeepers. The team scoring the greater number of goals after all players have completed all functions wins.

12

BEAT THAT PASS

FITNESS	½ Field or less	8 Players	1 Ball
			1 Cone

Goalkeeping
Passing
Throwing

Contributor: Jay Miller, Tampa University, Tampa, Florida 33606

Formation: Players X_1 through X_6 form a line. A cone is placed at a distance of ten to twenty yards in front of the line (the distance will depend upon how much sprinting is desired and the distance that the ball is being kicked). X_8 is about forty yards from start and X_7 is stationed near the cone.

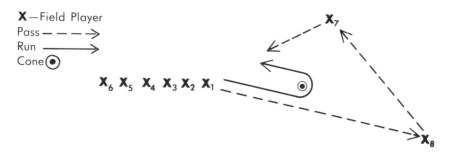

X—Field Player
Pass — — — →
Run ——————→
Cone⊙

X_6 X_5 X_4 X_3 X_2 X_1

X_7

X_8

Procedure: X_1 kicks the ball forward past X_8, if possible. X_1 then sprints around the cone and back to the start. Meanwhile X_8, who may be a field player or goalkeeper, retrieves the ball and attempts to hit X_1 or throw it to X_7 to hit X_1 before he returns to the start. If desired, score may be kept. Score one point for the sprinter if he gets back to start without being hit, or one point for the retrievers if the sprinter is hit before returning to start.

13

BEAT THE KEEPER

GOALKEEPING   10 yd. by 20 yd. Area   2 Players   1 Ball

                                           Goalkeeper   2 Cones

Heading

Formation: A goalkeeper is in a goal marked by two cones in the middle of the area. Two players, one with a ball, are at opposite ends of the area.

G—Goalkeeper
X—Field Player
Pass — — — ⇒
Shot ·········⇒
Ball •

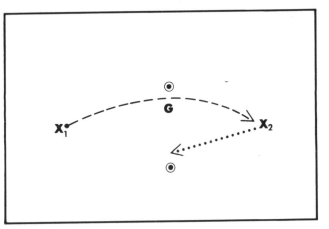

Procedure: X_1 throws or chips the ball to X_2 who heads the ball in an attempt to score on the goalkeeper. The goalkeeper should be facing X_1 and then turn to save the head shot by X_2. Later, the goalkeeper should be facing X_2 all the time. The goalkeeper gets a point for each save, while each field player gets a point for each score. The first player to score five points wins.

14

BEAT THEM ALL

OFFENSIVE AND DEFENSIVE TECHNIQUES	100 yd. by 15 yd. Area	8 to 12 Players	3 Balls
			8 Cones

Formation: A rectangular area one hundred yards by fifteen yards is marked with cones. Cones are placed at twenty yard intervals within the one hundred yard area. Offensive players line up at the entrance to the course. Defensive players position themselves between the width of the course at twenty yard intervals.

D—Defensive Player
O—Offensive Player
Dribble ∿∿∿>
Run ——————>
Cone ⊙

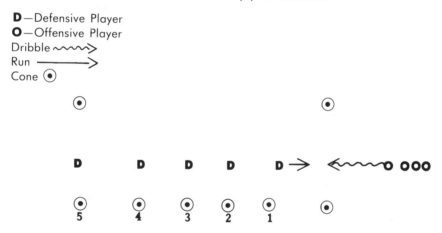

Procedure: An offensive player dribbles toward the first defensive player who advances from the first cone (twenty yards from start) and attempts to make a tackle. The offensive player attempts to beat the defensive player and, if successful, continues to advance to confront the next defensive player. The offensive player continues until he beats five defenders in order, or until he loses possession of the ball. After the offensive player completes his turn, he becomes a defensive player at cone five while all other defensemen move up one cone. The defensive player who started at cone one goes to the end of the waiting line of offensive players. Any player beating all five defenders wins.

15

BIG GOAL SHOOTING

SHOOTING	20 yd. by 30 yd. Area	8 or more Players	6 Balls
Offensive and Defensive Techniques		Goalkeepers	4 Cones

Contributor: *Al Albert, College of William and Mary, Williamsburg, Virginia 23185*

Formation: Two teams of equal numbers are opposite each other on their goal lines. Two players from each team are in the playing area. A coach, with a supply of balls, stands outside the middle of the area.

C —Coach
X —Field Player
Ball●
Cone ⊙

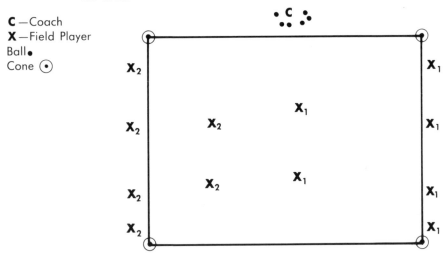

Procedure: The coach serves a ball into the middle of the area. Two players from each team play two vs two and attempt to score by shooting the ball, below waist height, over the opposing goal line.
All other players are goalkeepers who may use their hands but must stay on their goal line. The field players can pass balls back to their goalkeepers who can throw or roll the ball back to the players. Change players every two minutes. The first team to score ten goals wins.

16

BOMBARDMENT

CLEARING	¼ Field	12 Players	12 Balls
Passing (Chip)	& Penalty Area		

Formation: There are two teams of six players each. Six players, each with two balls, stand in different positions about twenty yards outside the penalty area. Six other players spread out within the penalty area.

D—Defensive Player
O—Offensive Player
Pass — — —$\rightarrow$
Ball •

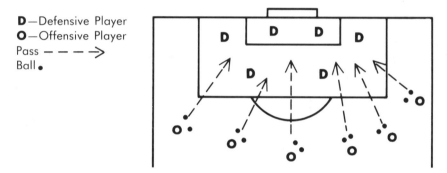

Procedure: The attackers alternate chipping balls into the penalty area in an attempt to score. The defenders try to prevent balls from entering the goal or landing in the penalty area by heading or clearing balls out of the area. The attackers score points as follows: Three points for a goal, two points for a ball touching ground in the goal area, and one point for a ball touching *ground* in the remainder of the penalty area. After twelve attempts, the teams change roles. The team scoring the most points wins.

17

BREAK IT DOWN

PASSING	15 yd. by 20 yd. Area	10 Players	1 Ball
			4 Cones
Defensive Techniques			4 Scrimmage Vests

Contributor: *John Rennie, Duke University, Durham, North Carolina 27706*

Formation: One offensive player is in the middle of the area, with five teammates spread around the area's boundaries. Four defenders, wearing vests, are located anywhere in the area.

D—Defensive Player
O—Offensive Player
Ball •
Cone ⊙

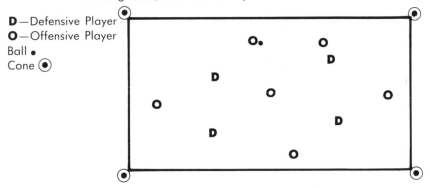

Procedure: The six offensive players play two touch keepaway against the four defenders. If a defender wins the ball, it is immediately returned to the attackers. Every two minutes, four offensive players change positions with the defenders, and a new offensive player goes into the middle.

The object is for the offensive players to make as many consecutive passes as possible. The middle offensive player counts the passes, while a defender counts the number of offensive breakdowns in each time period. Each group tries to beat the best number.

Variation:
• Vary area size
• Play one touch
• Add another offensive player
• Vary defensive tempo

18

CHIP AND DEFEND

CLEARING	½ Field	12 Players	6 Balls

Passing

Contributor: Jay Martin, Ohio Wesleyan University, Delaware, Ohio 43018

Formation: Six defensive players are in the penalty area. Six other players, each with a ball, are in the center circle. A fifteen yard square is marked at each sideline by mid-field.

D—Defensive Player
X—Field Player
Pass — — — —⟶
Ball ●

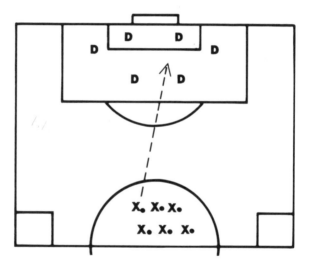

Procedure: The players in the center circle alternately chip balls into the penalty area. The players in the penalty area attempt to clear the balls toward the squares.
One point is scored for each ball landing in the penalty area and one point for each ball cleared into a square. The first group to score ten points wins.
Rotate the groups.

19 — CIRCLE TO SHOOT

SHOOTING	25 yds. in Front of a Goal	12 to 24 Players Goalkeepers	12 Balls Goal

Formation: One half of the group lines up behind one of the goal posts. The other half of the group spreads out and serves as retrievers. A feeder, about twenty yards from goal, spots or lobs the ball for the oncoming players. A cone is placed about five yards past the feeder. A goalkeeper is in the goal.

F —Feeder
G —Goalkeeper
O —Offensive Player
R —Retriever
Pass — — — ⟶
Run ⟶
Shot ·······▷
Ball •
Cone ⊙

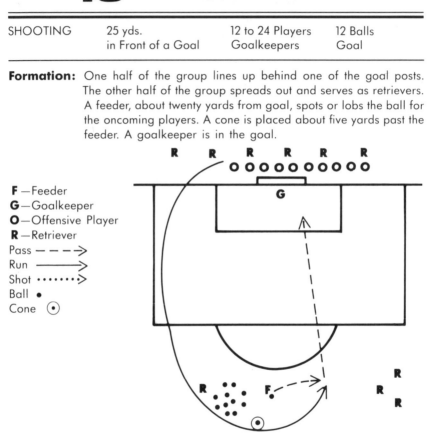

Procedure: The one half of the group that is shooting continuously runs in a large circle from the post, around the cone, and back behind the goal. After passing the cone, each shooter receives a ball from the feeder and shoots on goal. After a prescribed period of time (two minutes is suggested), the shooters become retrievers and the retrievers shoot. The team scoring the most goals during their offensive turn wins.

Variation: • Offensive players line up at the other post and shoot with other foot.
• The feeder lofts the ball higher and the shot is taken on the volley or headed on goal.

20

CONFINED ATTACK

OFFENSIVE TECHNIQUES	Penalty Area	8 Players	6 Balls
		Goalkeeper	Goal
Defensive Techniques Goalkeeping			

Contributor: *Gordie Howell, Rollins College, Winter Park, Florida 32789*

Formation: Four offensive players and four defensive players are in the penalty area. A goalkeeper is in the goal. A feeder with six balls stands outside the penalty area.

D—Defensive Player
F—Feeder
G—Goalkeeper
O—Offensive Player
Pass — — — →
Ball •

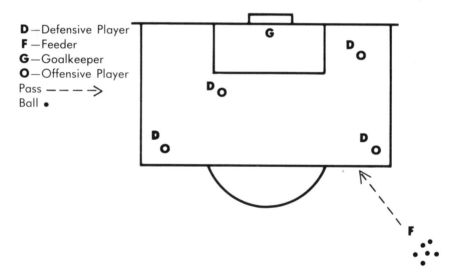

Procedure: Four offensive players attack against four defensive players for four minutes. The feeder serves another ball to an offensive player each time a ball goes out of play. Defenders must play man to man. The offensive group scoring the most goals in four minutes wins.

21

CONSECUTIVE PASSES

PASSING   ½ Field   12 or more Players   1 Ball

Defensive Techniques
Fitness

Contributor: *Schellas Hyndman, Eastern Illinois University, Charleston, Illinois 61020*

Formation: Two teams of six players each occupy one half of the soccer field. One team has a soccer ball.

D—Defensive Player
O—Offensive Player
Pass − − − −>
Run ─────>
Ball •

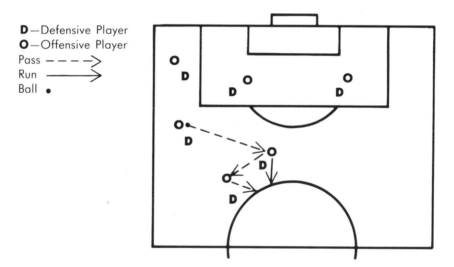

Procedure: The team in possession of the ball attempts to complete ten consecutive passes. A new count starts whenever ball possession changes. The first team to complete ten consecutive passes wins.

Variation: • Restrict individual control to one or two touch.
              • Restrict players to using only left or right foot.

22

CONTAIN

OFFENSIVE AND DEFENSIVE TECHNIQUES	5 yd. by 10 yd. Area	2 or more Players	1 Ball
			4 Cones

Formation: Four cones define a five-yard-by-ten-yard area. An offensive player with a ball enters at one end of the area. A defensive player at the other end is ready to confront the offensive player.

D—Defensive Player
O—Offensive Player
Dribble ∿∿⟶
Run ⟶
Ball •
Cone ⊙

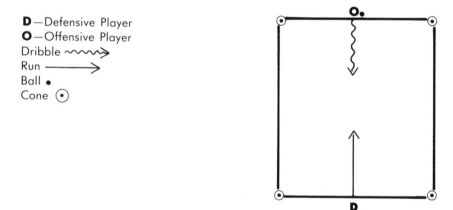

Procedure: At a signal, the offensive player enters the area. The defensive player confronts him but does not tackle. The object for the defensive player is to contain the offensive player within the area for ten seconds. The object for the offensive player is to exit the area within the allotted ten seconds.

23

CONTINUOUS PASS

PASSING	Any Area	8 to 20 Players	1 Ball

Contributor: *Robert A. Kullen, University of New Hampshire, Durham, New Hampshire, 03824*

Formation: Two lines of two or more players, about ten yards apart, are opposite and about ten yards from two other lines of players. The first player in one line has a soccer ball.

X —Field Player
Pass – – – →
Run ────→
Ball •

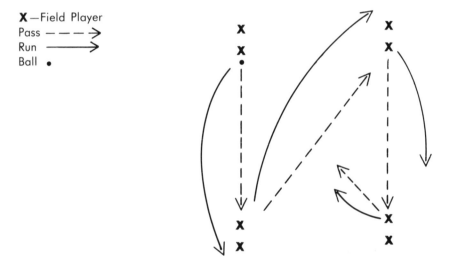

Procedure: The player with the ball makes a ground pass to the first player in the line opposite him and goes to the end of that line. The player receiving the ball makes a one-time pass to the first player in the diagonally opposite line and goes to the end of that line. This routine is repeated until an error is made, after which the player making the mistake restarts the routine. Count the number of consecutive one-touch passes. Set a goal to reach or try to improve the best performance each time.

Variation:
- Designate foot to be used.
- Vary the distance between the lines.
- Make it two touch for passes in the air.

24

CORNER BALL

| OFFENSIVE AND DEFENSIVE TECHNIQUES | 40 yd. by 40 yd. Area | 8 to 16 Players | 1 Ball |

Contributor: *Tom Taylor, West Essex High School, North Caldwell, New Jersey 07006*

Formation: There are four teams of two to four players each. Each team occupies one of the four corner squares of the area. A ball is in the center of the area.

X—Field Player
Ball •

X_1 X_1			X_2 X_2
		•	
X_4 X_4			X_3 X_3

Procedure: On a signal, all players move to gain possession of the ball. The team winning the ball tries to get it back to their square while the other players defend and attempt to take the ball away. The first team to get the ball to their square wins.

25

COUNTER ATTACK

OFFENSIVE	Full Field	8 to 24 Players	6 Balls
AND DEFENSIVE TECHNIQUES		2 Goalkeepers	4 Cones

Contributor: *Will Myers, William Paterson College, Wayne, New Jersey 07470*

Formation: Cones set three yards apart mark goals five yards in from the midfield line. Full-size goals are at the ends of the field. A goalkeeper is in each full-size goal and three defenders are on each endline. Four offensive players stand on an imaginary line extending across the field from the goals marked by cones.

G—Goalkeeper
D—Defensive Player
O—Offensive Player
Ball •
Cone ⊙

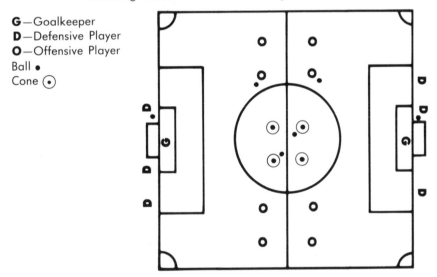

Procedure: Play starts by each offensive unit attempting to score at the regulation goal. Defensive players winning the ball attempt to score upon the unguarded midfield goal. Ten tries are attempted by the offense. A "try" is completed when the ball goes over the endline, sideline or the imaginary line near midfield. The team (offensive or defensive) scoring the most goals upon completion of ten tries initiated by the offense wins.

Variation: • Use a goalie plus two defenders vs. three offensive players.

26

CRAB DRIBBLE

DRIBBLING	Center Circle	10 Players	5 Balls
Fitness			
Tackling			

Formation: Five players, each with a ball, stand in the center circle. Five defenders, in "crab" position (supine position with body held off the floor by the hands and feet), are also in the center circle.

D—Defensive Player
O—Offensive Player
Dribble ∿∿∿⟩
Ball •

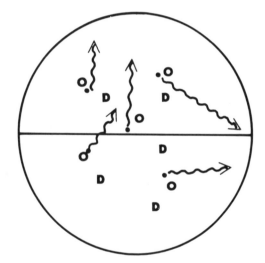

Procedure: At a signal, the attackers dribble within the center circle. They continue dribbling for two minutes. The defenders, in crab position, try to kick the balls out of the circle. Once an attacker's ball is kicked out of the circle, the attacker is eliminated. After two minutes, the players reverse roles. The team that kicks the most balls out of the circle wins.

Variation: • The team with the most dribblers remaining at the end of the time period wins.

27

CRAB SOCCER

FITNESS	Gymnasium	10 Players	1 Ball
			2 Small Goals

Formation: Two teams of five players each are in their respective half court. All players are in "crab" position; i.e., in a supine position with the body held off the floor by the hands and feet. A ball is at midcourt. One indoor-size goal is on each end line.

X—Field Player
Ball •

Procedure: On a signal, one player from each team attempts to gain possession of the ball. This is a five vs. five game except that the ball may only be played when a player is in the crab position. It is a foul to play the ball with any part of the body on the floor except the hands and feet. The most goals in a set time period win.

Variation: • Players are in prone position on all fours.

28

CRAB TACKLE

TACKLING	Center Circle	8 or more Players	4 or more Balls
Dribbling			

Formation: Two teams of equal numbers are in the center circle. Each player on one team has a ball. The other players assume a crab-walk position (i.e., a supine position on all four limbs).

D—Defensive Player
O—Offensive Player
Dribble 〰〰⟩
Ball •

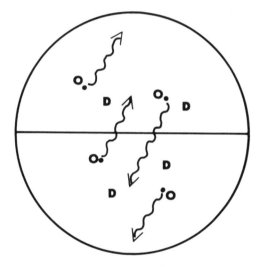

Procedure: The players with the balls dribble within the circle. The other players attempt to slide, tackle or flick the balls out of the circle while in a crab-walk position. They must be on all four limbs when making contact with an opponent. After all the balls have been kicked out of the circle, the players switch positions. The team that kicks all the balls out in the least time is the winner.

Variation: • After a dribbler has lost the ball, he becomes a "crab." The last dribbler is the winner.

29 - DAISYCUTTER
30 - DENY THROUGH PASS

PASSING   10 yd. by 10 yd. Areas   2 or more Players   1 Ball per Pair

Formation: Two players with one ball are in each square.

X—Field Player
Pass — — —>
Ball •

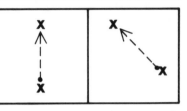

Procedure: How many "daisycutter" passes can be made in thirty seconds without the ball going out of the square? A "daisycutter" pass is one without a bounce and so cuts the daisies in its path.

Variation: • If the ball goes out of the square, the count goes to zero.
• If a ball is passed with a bounce, the count goes to zero.

PASSING   Defensive Techniques   10 yard by 10 yard Area   6 Players   1 Ball

Contributor: I. M. Ibrahim, Clemson University, Clemson, South Carolina 29631

Formation: Four offensive players position themselves in a square about ten to fifteen yards apart. Two defensive players are within the square formed by the offensive players.

D—Defensive Player
O—Offensive Player
Pass — — — >
Ball •

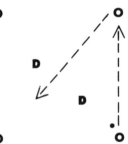

Procedure: Offensive players pass the ball among themselves and score a point if a through pass (to the player diagonally across) is completed. Defensive players score a point each time they intercept a pass.

Variation: • (Two touch) Offensive players may control and pass.
• (One touch) Offensive players must pass without controlling the ball.

31

DISTANCE KICKING

KICKING	½ Field and Extended Area Beyond Touch Lines	10 to 20 Players	1 Ball
Receiving			

Formation: Players are divided into two teams. Players spread out along the sideline of one-half of the field or similar area.

X —Field Player
Pass — — — →
Ball •

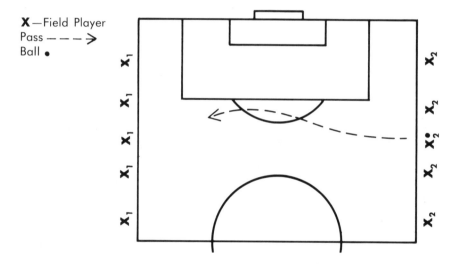

Procedure: One team starts with a kick. The team on the opposite side of the field must, if possible, return the ball while it is still moving. Otherwise, the ball is kicked from where it comes to rest. If the ball leaves the field over a line other than the sideline, it is returned from the point where it went out of bounds. The object of the game is for one team to advance so far that they play the ball from the outside of the opponent's sideline.

32

DISTRIBUTION ACCURACY

PASSING 20 yd. by 20 yd. Area 2 or more Players 4 Balls

3 Cones

Formation: A feeder faces a field player who is fifteen yards away. Cones are placed ten yards in front of the defender.

D—Defensive Player
F—Feeder
Pass — — — →
Ball •
Cone (•)

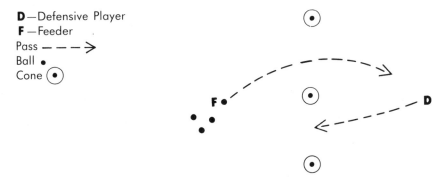

Procedure: The feeder serves the ball to the defensive player and calls out the direction of the target cone, i.e., right, left, center. One point is awarded if the ball is passed in the proper direction. Three points are awarded if the ball hits the proper target. Each defender gets ten tries. The player with the highest score after all players have had a turn wins.

33-DODGEBALL
34-DRIBBLE FOR COURAGE

PASSING	Center Circle	12 Players	6 Balls

Formation: Six players, each with a ball, spread out around the center circle. Six other players are in the circle.

X—Field Player
Ball •

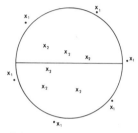

Procedure: On a signal, the players on the outside of the circle begin kicking the balls at the players in the circle who try to evade the kicks. Kicking continues for a set time period (one or two minutes). A player hit below the waist is out of the game. After time expires, the teams change roles and the game continues. The team with the most players remaining after one or more periods wins.

DRIBBLING	Center Circle	10 to 20 Players	1 Ball per Player

Contributor: Robert E. Nye, The College of Wooster, Wooster, Ohio 44691

Formation: Players spread out around the center circle. Each player has a ball.

X—Field Player
Dribble ⌇⌇⌇⟹
Ball •

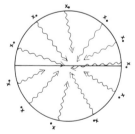

Procedure: On a signal, each player dribbles at top speed to the opposite side of the circle. Each player must keep control of his own ball. The last player to reach the opposite side, and any players losing ball control, dribble one lap around the field.

35

DRIBBLE RELAY

FITNESS	35 yd. by 20 yd. Area	2 to 12 Players	2 Balls
Dribbling			12 cones

Formation: Two groups of players line up in relay fashion and face a course thirty yards long. Cones are placed at five-yard intervals in front of a starting line. Two players run the course at a time.

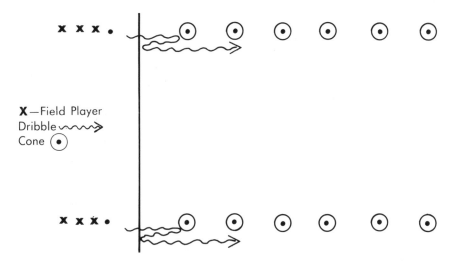

Procedure: The first player in each line dribbles as fast as possible to the first cone and back to the start. He then dribbles to the second cone and back to the start, etc., until the entire course is completed, after which the next two players go, and so on until players complete the course.

Variation: • The course may be run without a ball.
• The run may be timed, creating competition between players and motivation to achieve personal best times.

36

DRIBBLE TAG

| DRIBBLING | Penalty Area | 5 to 20 Players | 1 Ball per Player |

Contributor: Dan Harris, University of Wisconsin-Milwaukee, Milwaukee, Wisconsin 53201

Formation: Each player, with a ball, stands in the penalty area.

X—Field Player
Dribble ~~~⟩
Ball •

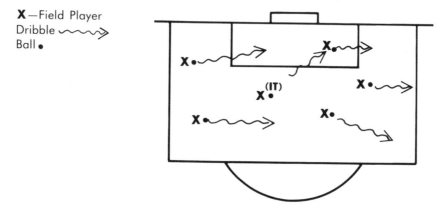

Procedure: The game is played like a game of tag, except that each player is dribbling a ball at his feet. One player who is "it" chases the other players and tags anyone he can. However, he must maintain control of his ball while tagging. A tagged player becomes "it" and continues the game but may not tag the player who tagged him. A player is "it" if he loses control of his ball and it goes out of bounds. All players must continue moving even if not being chased. The coach should call out the name of the "it" player.

Variation: More than one player can be "it."

37

FIRST TIME SHOOTING

SHOOTING	Penalty Area	5 Players	6 Balls
Fitness		Goalkeeper	1 Cone
Goalkeeping			Goal

Formation: A cone is placed eighteen yards out from the center of the goal. One player stands about three yards behind the cone, a second player is positioned about ten yards to the right of the cone with three balls, and a third player is about ten yards to the left of the cone also with three balls. A goalkeeper is in goal. Two retrievers stand behind the goal.

F —Feeder
G —Goalkeeper
O —Offensive Player
R —Retriever
Pass - - - →
Run ——→
Shot ······→
Cone ⊙

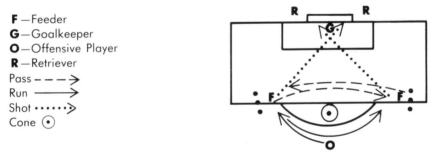

Procedure: The feeder on the right side passes the ball past and slightly in front of the cone. The shooter makes a run to the left of the cone and shoots first time. The shooter then runs in a semi-circle behind and then to the right of the cone to meet a pass from the feeder on the left side of the cone and again shoots first time. Retrievers and the goalkeeper return balls to feeders. The game continues for one minute, after which each player, except the goalkeeper, moves to the next position in a clockwise direction. The player scoring the most goals in one minute wins.

Variation: • The shooter may remain in his position for longer than one minute.
• Feeders may serve high balls for head shots.

38

FIVE vs FIVE AND GOALKEEPERS

OFFENSIVE AND DEFENSIVE TECHNIQUES	Penalty Area	20 Players	1 Ball
			Vests

Shooting

Formation: Two teams (X_1 and X_2) of ten men each are differentiated by colored vests. Five players from each team are in the center of the penalty area. Five players from each team are on the endline of the penalty area.

X—Field Player

Ball ●

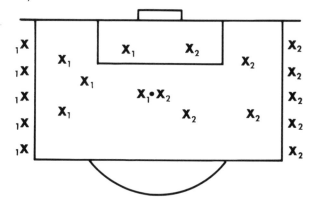

Procedure: A five vs. five game is played within the penalty area. To score a goal the ball must pass beyond the endline of the penalty area lower than waist level. Players on the endline serve as goalkeepers. After five minutes of play, goalkeepers become field players and field players become goalkeepers. The game continues for five more minutes. The team scoring the greater number of goals wins.

39 – FIVE vs FIVE vs FIVE

OFFENSIVE AND DEFENSIVE TECHNIQUES	Full Field	15 Players	1 Ball
		2 Goalkeepers	Vests

Contributor: *Bud Lewis, Wilmington College, Wilmington, Ohio 45177*

Formation: There are three teams (X_1, X_2, X_3) of five players each wearing different colored vests. Two teams are spread out in one half field and a third team is in the other half field. A goalkeeper defends each goal.

G—Goalkeeper   **X**—Field Player   Ball •

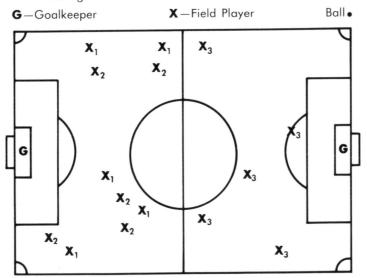

Procedure: The X_1 team starts the game by attacking the goal defended by the X_2 team. If X_2 wins the ball, they must get it across midfield while X_1 tries to prevent this and get back on attack. Should X_2 succeed in getting the ball over mid-field, they attack the goal defended by the X_3 team. Play continues in the same fashion with a different team trying to cross mid-field each time. If one team scores, they maintain possession and restart the game attacking the opposite goal.

Variation: • Different size squads can be used to emphasize different situations e.g., one vs. one vs. one, two vs. two vs. two, etc.

40

FOLLOW THE LEADER

FITNESS	Any Area	2 or more Players	None

Contributor: *Ernie Unger, Paramus High School, Paramus, New Jersey 07652*

Formation: Unlimited number of players line up in double file behind two leaders.

X—Field Player X_1 X_1 X_1 X_1 X_1

X_2 X_2 X_2 X_2 X_2

Procedure: Players follow the designated leaders around an open area and imitate their activities. Except where indicated, movement continues. The activities to be completed over a two-mile course follow:
- jog forward
- jog, slapping heels as you go
- jog backwards
- pretend to pick up a penny on each third step (straight legs)
- jog sideward
- leapfrog over partner
- hop forward with both feet together
- race your partner—sprint
- pretend to pick up gold coins every 5 seconds (straight legs)
- clean your cleats (hold one foot in hand every third step)
- alternately grab heels with hands and walk
- jog sideward (step over)
- straight leg kicks at extended hands
- jog backwards
- touch inside of heels as you jog
- one foot hop race with your partner
- river straddle (walk with wide stance—one foot on each shore)
- river bank hop (side to side jumps in forward direction)
- lean on your partner jog (shoulder to shoulder)
- lift thighs very high as you jog
- forward rolls
- sit down, get up (take several steps before repeating)
- gorilla stroll (arms hanging down, etc.)
- jump for the sky

- fly wheel (take both hands of partner and hurl him forward and around)
- drag your partner (one man resists)
- animal walk (on all fours)
- raise thigh-rotate hip-step forward
- heel walk
- tip-toe through the tulips (jog on toes)
- race your partner backwards
- race him sidewards
- giant steps
- pump the well (back-to-back, lock arms, and alternate lifting)
- carry your partner on your back (piggy back)
- pretend to jump for the ball with partner
- wheelbarrow race (one partner holds ankles of other who walks on hands)
- human chain (grab ankle of man in front of you and walk)
- cross over step
- spin around in a circle and sprint five steps
- goose step march
- mini steps (heel to toe)
- push the stalled truck (get behind your partner, place your hands on his back and push, he leans back)
- underhanded applause (clap hands under legs on every step)

Variation: • After each activity, the next pair in line move up one position and become the leaders.

41

FOLLOW THE PASS

| PASSING
Dribbling
Receiving | Center Circle | 10 to 30 Players | 1 to 5 Balls |

Contributor: John Makuvek, Moravian College, Bethlehem, Pennsylvania 18018

Formation: The players spread out around the center circle. One player has a soccer ball.

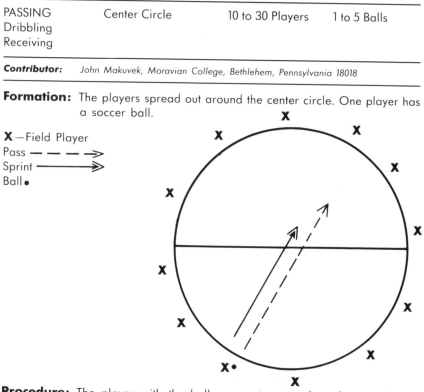

X —Field Player
Pass — — — ⟶
Sprint ⟶
Ball •

Procedure: The player with the ball passes to any other player and then sprints to that player's spot. The players receiving the ball continue the passing and sprinting. Passes should be one or two touch. After awhile add more balls up to a maximum of five. The object of the game is to make as many consecutive passes as possible without an error, without any balls touching another ball or player, and without players running into each other.

Variation:
- Ground passes only.
- Air passes only.
- Dribble to the other player.
- Dribble halfway across and then pass to the other player.

42 – FOUR CORNERS

OFFENSIVE	½ Field	10 to 20 Players	1 Balls
AND DEFENSIVE			
TECHNIQUES			8 Cones
Goalkeeping			

Contributor: *Bill Coulthart, Jacksonville University, Box 30, Jacksonville, Florida 32211*

Formation: Two teams of equal numbers are in half field. A player on one team has a soccer ball. Four goals, marked by cones six feet apart, are positioned in the extreme corners of the field so that they face the center.

X—Field Player
Ball ●
Cone ⊙

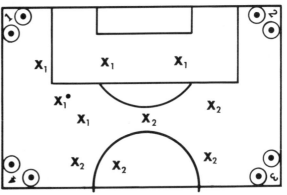

Procedure: Each team defends two adjacent goals; X_1 defends goals one and two and X_2 defends goals three and four. The game is played as in regulation soccer except that teams can attack the two opposite corner goals. The team scored against restarts play immediately from in front of the goal scored upon. The first team to score ten goals wins.

Variation:
- Players may touch the ball no more than one or two times in succession
- To involve goalkeepers, make a goal eight yards wide in the center of the field for the goalkeeper to defend. The goalkeeper may move only on his goal line. Teams must beat the goalkeeper in the center goal before attacking a corner goal. Any loss of possession requires a team to beat the goalkeeper again. The goalkeeper distributes any saves to either team in a corner of the field.

43

FOUR CORNERS SOCCER

PASSING   30 yd. by 40 yd. Area   12 Players   1 Ball

8 Cones

Formation: There are two teams of six players each in a small field with four goals. The goals are cone high, four yards wide, and placed five yards in from the corners.

X—Field Player
Ball •
Cone ⊙

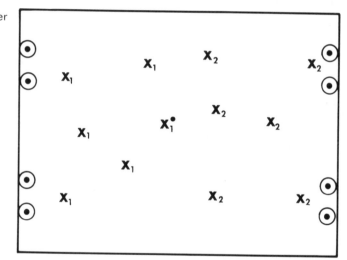

Procedure: This is a six vs. six game in which each team has two goals to attack and two to defend.

The coach can "condition" the game to emphasize short passing: e.g.
- Three, two, or one touch restriction.
- All passes must be beneath waist height.
- A team must make five passes before trying to score.
- All passes must go forward or backwards only.
- If a player turns the ball over, he comes out of the game for one minute or until his team makes five passes.

44

FOUR GOAL—FOUR BALL SOCCER

OFFENSIVE AND DEFENSIVE TECHNIQUES	Full Field	8 to 20 Players	4 Balls
		4 Goalkeepers	4 Goals
Fitness			

Contributor: *Ron McEachen, Middlebury College, Middlebury, Vermont 05753*

Formation: Two team of equal numbers set up as in a regulation game. A player on one team has a soccer ball. There are four goals; one regulation goal on each end line and one portable goal on each sideline at mid-field. A goalkeeper is in each goal.

G—Goalkeeper
X—Field Player
Ball •

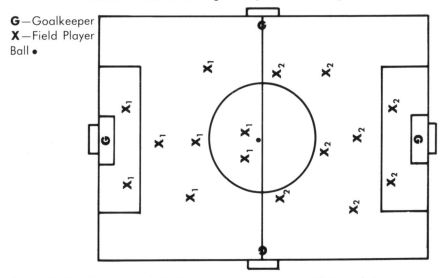

Procedure: This is a regulation soccer match except that each team may score in two goals, and more than one ball may be used. To start, each team attacks the appropriate regulation goal and one sideline goal. The sideline goal assignment can be changed periodically. Extra balls are put into play, one at a time. The game becomes one of pressure and fun as the third and fourth balls are added.

45

FOUR vs FOUR PLUS TWO

OFFENSIVE AND DEFENSIVE TECHNIQUES	30 yd. by 30 yd. Area	10 Players	1 Ball
			2 Small Goals

Formation: Two teams of four players each are positioned in the area. There are two extra players. One of the players has a ball. There are two indoor size goals.

M—Midfield Player
X—Field Player
Ball .

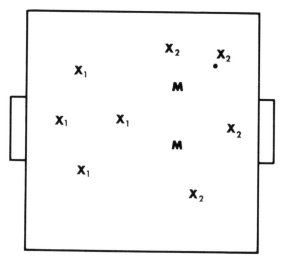

Procedure: This is a four vs. four game with two floating players who play for the side in possession. The floaters might wear different colored vests to denote their roles. The team scoring the most goals in a set time period wins.

46

FOUR vs FOUR PRESSURE

OFFENSIVE AND DEFENSIVE TECHNIQUES	Penalty Area	12 Players	8 Balls
Goalkeeping Shooting		Goalkeeper	

Contributor: William G. Rogers, Babson College, Babson Park, Massachusetts 02157

Formation: Four attackers compete against four defenders and a goalkeeper in the penalty area. Two players, with a supply of balls, are located at the sides of the area, and serve as feeders. Two other players are outside the top of the area.

D—Defensive Player
G—Goalkeeper
F—Feeder
O—Offensive Player
X—Field Player
Ball •

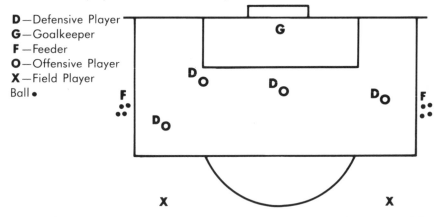

Procedure: One of the feeders crosses or passes a ball into the area and the players compete against each other until a goal is scored or the ball is cleared out of the area. The players at the top of the area shoot or pass balls cleared their way back into the area. Otherwise, one of the feeders will make another cross or pass. The four offensive players scoring the most goals in a set time period win. All players are rotated after a specified period of time.

Variation:
- Change the number of players in the area.
- Use a strict man-to-man defense.
- Vary the types of crosses and passes.

47

FOUR vs FOUR SHOOT OR SPRINT

PASSING   20 yd. by 20 yd. Area   8 Players   1 Ball

4 Cones

Fitness   8 Scrimmage
                                                              Vests

Contributor: Eugene Chyzowych, Columbia High School, Maplewood, New Jersey 07040

Formation: Two teams of four players each, wearing different colored scrimmage vests, are in a twenty yard by twenty yard grid. A player on one team, X_2, has a soccer ball. There are two goals; each goal formed by two cones, two yards apart.

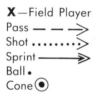

X—Field Player
Pass — — —⟫
Shot ⋯⋯⋯⋗
Sprint ——⟫
Ball •
Cone ⊙

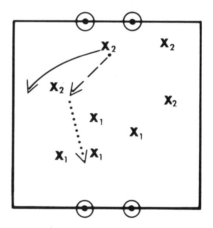

Procedure: This is a four vs. four game with a restriction that a player making a pass must sprint five yards in any direction immediately after the pass. However, a player does not have to sprint after taking a shot on goal. The game can be played for a set time period or number of goals.

Variation: • Play one, two or unlimited touch.
                  • Advance ball only by using hands.

48

GET TO A CORNER

OFFENSIVE AND DEFENSIVE TECHNIQUES	10 yd. by 10 yd. Area	2 Players	1 Ball
			4 Cones

Passing

Formation: The four corners of the area are marked by cones. X_1, with a ball, is at one corner, and X_2 is at the diagonally opposite corner.

X—Field Player
Pass — — →
Run ——→
Ball.
Cone ◉

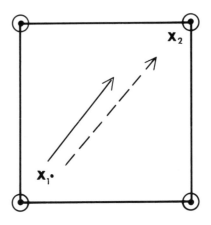

Procedure: X_1 starts play by passing to X_2. When X_2 receives the ball, X_1 moves to challenge. The player with the ball tries to touch the opposite cone or either side cone with the ball. Score ten points for the cross cones and five points for the side cones. If a defender gets the ball, he goes on attack immediately. After a cone is touched, the players return to their corners. The player who received the ball the first time now passes the ball. The player with the most points after a pre-set time period, or the player who earns a pre-set point total first, is the winner.

49

GIVE AND GO

PASSING	10 yd. by 20 yd. Area	8 Players	1 Ball

Formation: Three players spread out along each side of the area and are available to assist the attacker beat the defender.

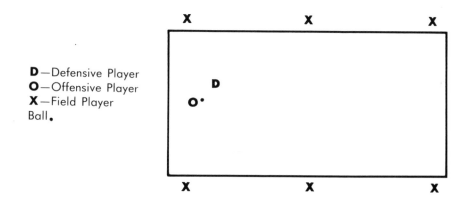

D—Defensive Player
O—Offensive Player
X—Field Player
Ball.

Procedure: O looks for give and go (wall pass) opportunities with any of the outside players (X) as he tries to beat D and reach the other end of the area. If successful, he turns and attacks D in the other direction. If unsuccessful, O and D exchange roles. Play should be continuous. Rotate the players after a set time period. The player who beats his opponent the greatest number of times wins.

50

GOAL BATTLE

SHOOTING   20 yd. by 20 yd. Area   5 Players   5 Balls

2 Goals

Contributor: Lawrence J. Zelz, Gettysburg College, Gettysburg, Pennsylvania 17325

Formation: Two field players stand in the middle of the playing area. A feeder, with five balls, stands to the side of the area. A retriever is behind each goal.

F —Feeder
R —Retriever
X —Field Player
Ball •

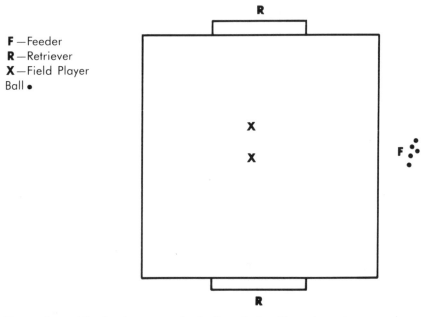

Procedure: The feeder serves the ball so that neither player has an advantage as each attempts to win the ball and shoot on the goal. Serves should be varied in height, speed, etc. The winner is the player with the most shots on goal or most goals after five serves.

Variation: • Goalkeepers may be added.

51

GOALKEEPER DISTANCE THROW

GOALKEEPING   Length of Soccer Field   2 Goalkeepers   1 Ball

Formation: Two goalkeepers face each other forty yards apart with the center stripe of the field between them.

G—Goalkeeper

Pass — — — →

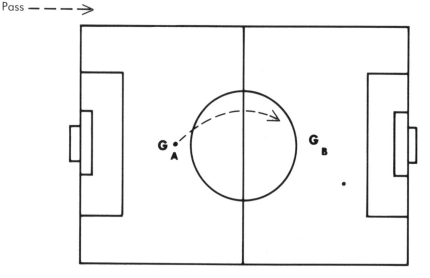

Procedure: Goalkeeper A throws the ball to goalkeeper B. If goalkeeper B fumbles, he moves back ten yards. Goalkeeper B throws back to goalkeeper A. Each player attempts to drive the other over the end line of the field. If the ball goes over the receiver's head, it is returned to the point where it first touched the ground.

Variation: • Goalkeepers punt or drop kick

52

GOALKEEPERS ALL

OFFENSIVE AND DEFENSIVE TECHNIQUES Goalkeeping	Penalty Area	10 to 20 Players	4 Balls

Formation: Players are divided into two teams (X_1 and X_2) of equal numbers. Players are numbered sequentially from one through the number of players on the team. One team spreads out on one endline of the penalty area, and the other team is on the opposite endline. A feeder with a supply of balls is between the two teams and outside the area.

F —Feeder
X —Field Player
Ball •

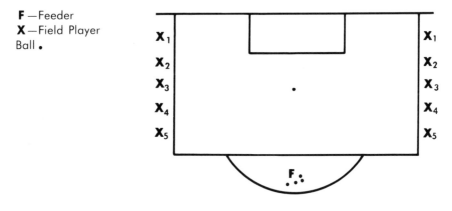

Procedure: The feeder calls out a number and the player from each team who has been assigned that number sprints to the center. A one vs. one game is played. The object is to score by shooting the ball across the opposite line. All players on the line function as goalkeepers. The ball must be driven below waist level. The team scoring the greater number of goals in a set time period wins.

Variation: • Call more than one number creating two vs. two, three vs. three, etc., situations.

53

GOALKEEPERS GAME

| GOALKEEPING | Full Field | 6 or more Goalkeepers | 1 Ball |

Fitness

Formation: Three or more goalkeepers line up in each half of the field.

G—Goalkeeper
Ball ●

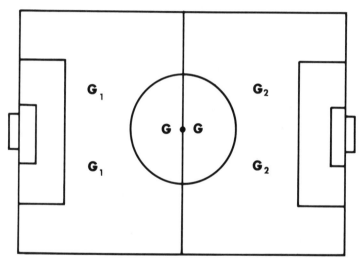

Procedure: The game is started with a basketball style jump ball. Players advance the ball by throwing and catching. No more than three steps may be taken by the player with the ball before the pass. Defensive players attempt to intercept. Goals may be scored only by a drop kick. The team scoring the greater number of goals within a given time period wins.

54

HALF-COURT SOCCER

OFFENSIVE AND DEFENSIVE TECHNIQUES	Penalty Area	8 Players	1 Ball
		Goalkeeper	Vests

Formation: Eight players, four to a team, are inside a penalty area. Teams wear different colored vests. A goalkeeper is in goal.

G—Goalkeeper
X—Field Player
Ball.

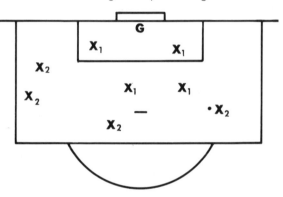

Procedure: The game is four vs. four played like half-court basketball. Either team can shoot at any time. After the goalkeeper makes a save, he puts the ball back in play and either team may gain possession. However, if the team that had possession before the goalkeeper save gains possession, they must take the ball back to the penalty mark before advancing it and taking another shot. If the ball goes over the endline after last being touched by an offensive player, the game is restarted by the defensive team with a throw in from the side of the area. If the ball goes over the endline having last been touched by a defensive player, play is resumed with an offensive corner kick. The team scoring the most goals in a set time period wins.

55

HANDBALL

SUPPORT	Penalty Area	14 to 22 Players	1 Ball

Contributor: Nick Mykulak, Stevens Institute of Technology, Hoboken, New Jersey 07030

Formation: Two teams of equal numbers are spread within the penalty area. A player on one team has a ball.

X—Field Player
Ball •

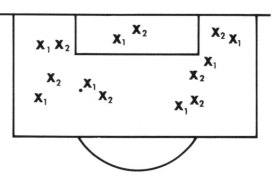

Procedure: This games is played by throwing and catching the ball. The object is for one team to make a specified number of consecutive passes before the ball is intercepted by the opposing team or thrown out of the area. Defending players may not grab ball out of an opponent's hands. The defending team takes possession of any deflected or dropped ball. The player with the ball may not take more than three steps. Depending on ability level, five to ten consecutive passes equal one goal.

Variation: • Use a smaller area such as center circle.
• Increase or decrease the number of players.

56

HANDICAP SOCCER

PASSING	30 yd. by 30 yd. Area	8 Players	1 Ball
			4 Cones

Offensive and Defensive
Techniques

Formation: One team of five players and another team of three players are in the area. One team has a ball. The goals are five feet wide marked by cones.

X—Field Player
Ball •
Cone

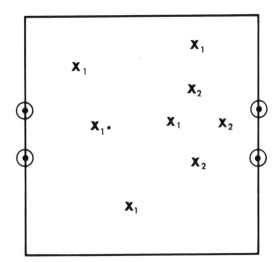

Procedure: The teams play a regulation type game except that, while the team of three players has no restrictions, the team of five must make one touch passes.

57

HEADERS AND CROSSES

HEADING	Penalty Area	12 or more Players 5 Balls
Passing		Goalkeeper

Formation: There are two teams, X_1 and X_2, of equal numbers. A player on X_1, with a supply of balls, is located to the side of and just outside the penalty area. The other X_1 players are in a line just outside the goal area. The X_2 players stand behind the goal to retrieve balls. A goalkeeper is in goal.

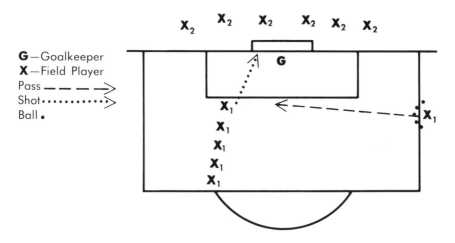

G—Goalkeeper
X—Field Player
Pass — — — —>
Shot •••••••••>
Ball •

Procedure: Each player on each team takes turns at serving crosses to each of his teammates to try headers at goal. Points are scored as follows:
- Two points for each goal.
- One point for each attempt which requires a save.
- No points for any attempt off target.
- Minus one point for any cross that cannot be headed.

The team with the most points after a set time or number of attempts wins.

Variation: • Make crosses from both sides of the penalty area.

58

HEADING SOCCER

HEADING	60 yd. by 40 yd. Area	6 to 9 Players per Team	1 Ball
Fitness			2 Small Goals

Contributor: *William De Peppe, Freehold Township High School, Freehold, New Jersey 07728*

Formation: Two teams of equal numbers spread out in the area. A player on one team has a soccer ball.

X—Field Player
Ball **.**

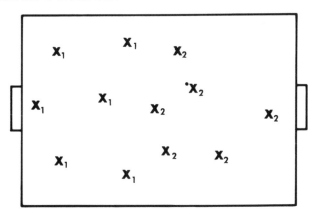

Procedure: The team in possession moves on attack and tries to score. The teams move up and down the field by players heading the ball to teammates. The ball may be caught and tossed for another header, or there can be continuous heading. The opponents may intercept the ball with their hands and start their attack. A ball touching the ground goes to the opponents. Goals are scored only by heading and play continues immediately.

Variation: • Play the game with regulation goals and goalkeepers.

59

HEAD VOLLEYBALL

HEADING	Center Circle	14 to 22 Players	1 Ball
		2 Goalkeepers	
Control			

Contributor: *Marc Whitehouse, Gordon College, Wenham, Massachusetts 01984*

Formation: One goalkeeper and several field players occupy each side of a center circle.

G—Goalkeeper
X—Field Player
Ball.

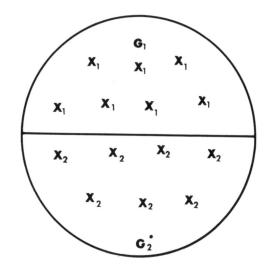

Procedure: The goalkeeper puts the ball in play by tossing it to the opposing side of the circle. Once put in play, the ball may touch the ground once on each side without penalty. The ball must cross the center line with a header, or a reaction rebound off a sharp header. Stress heading down. As in volleyball, you get three touches to a side, and no player may play the ball two times in succession. The first team to score fifteen points wins.

60

HUNTERS AND RABBITS

DRIBBLING	Center Circle	12 or more Players	12 Balls
Fitness			

Formation: Two groups of six players each are located in the center circle. Each player in one group has a ball. Extra balls are scattered just outside the circle.

X—Field Player
Dribble 〰〰➤
Ball •

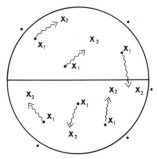

Procedure: The players with the balls are the hunters and the other players are the rabbits. At a signal, the hunters must chase the rabbits while dribbling the ball and "shoot" them by hitting them with a ball. The rabbits try to evade being hit. After being hit, a rabbit picks up a loose ball from outside the circle and joins the hunters until one winning rabbit remains.

61

IN PLAY

OFFENSIVE AND DEFENSIVE TECHNIQUES	10 yd. by 10 yd. Area	2 Players	1 Ball
Fitness			6 Cones

THE SOCCER GAMES BOOK

Formation: Two players are within a ten yard by ten yard area. One player has a ball. Two cones in the center of the area designate a two yard wide goal.

X—Field Player
Ball •
Cone ⊙

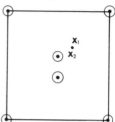

Procedure: The player with possession of the ball is on offense, the other is on defense. The ball is always in play even after a goal when both players chase the ball in an attempt to be on offense. The winner is the first player to score a designated number of goals or the player scoring the greater number of goals in a prescribed time period.

62 – JUGGLING RELAY

JUGGLING   ½ Field   8 or more Players   1 Ball per team
Dribbling
Fitness

Formation: Two or more teams of four players each line up on one sideline about five yards apart. The first player in each line has a ball.

X—Field Player
Dribble ～～～⟶
Sprint ——⟹
Ball•

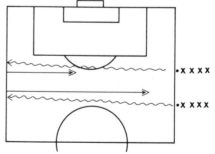

Procedure: At a signal, the first player in each line begins executing a set number of juggles. After completing the juggling, each player dribbles at top speed to the opposite side line, picks up the ball, sprints back, and hands the ball to the next player in line who repeats the routine.

63

KEEP AWAY

PASSING	10 yd. by 10 yd. Area	3 to 6 Players	1 Ball
			4 Cones
Control			

Contributor: Bill Shellenberger, Lynchburg College, Lynchburg, Virginia 24501

Formation: The four corners of the area are marked by cones. One offensive player is at each cone and two defenders are within the area. One offensive player has a ball.

D—Defensive Player
O—Offensive Player
Pass — — — >
Ball •
Cone ⊙

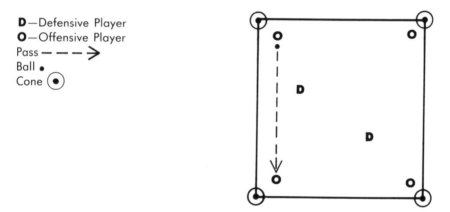

Procedure: Two, three, or four corners can be occupied by offensive players who try to keep the ball away from the defenders by square or diagonal passes. If a defender intercepts a pass, he changes places with the player whose pass he intercepts. The object of the game is to complete as many passes as possible with each group trying to beat the previous high.

Variation:
• Vary the number of defensive players.
• A time period, which can vary, can be set.

64

KEEP AWAY (3 vs 1)

PASSING	10 yd. by 10 yd. Area	4 Players	1 Ball
			4 Cones
Fitness			

Formation: Three players, one with a soccer ball, stand on the boundaries of a ten yard area. One player is in the middle of the area.

D—Defensive Player
O—Offensive Player
Pass — — — →
Ball •
Cone (●)

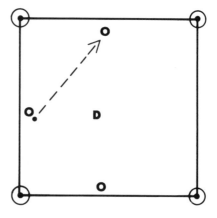

Procedure: The player in the middle tries to intercept the ball while the outside players pass it around. If the middle player touches the ball, the outside player who last played the ball goes to the middle. If a team makes five consecutive passes without losing possession to the middle man, the middle man gets a negative point. The loser is the one with the highest number of negative points after a pre-set time.

Variation: • Increase the number of passes to ten or fifteen.

65 – KEEP AWAY (4 vs 2)

PASSING	Penalty Area	6 Players	1 Ball

Movement Without the Ball

Contributor: *Ronald Broadbent, State University of New York at Brockport, Brockport, New York 14420*

Formation: Six players are in a penalty area or similar space. Four players are on offense, and two players are on defense.

D—Defensive Player
O—Offensive Player
Ball •

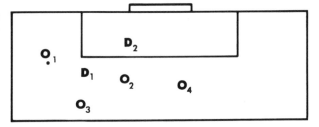

Procedure: The six players pair up as partners. They remain partners throughout the game. Assume O_1 and O_2 are partners: O_3 and O_4 are partners: and D_1 and D_2 are partners. To start the game, two sets of partners combine, giving four players on offense. The remaining pair will be the defense. The wall pass, through pass, square pass, chip pass, and sideline pass are utilized with constant movement within the area. The four offensive players attempt to keep the ball away from the two defensive players, and in the process are trying to achieve ten consecutive passes without the defense controlling the ball. Each time ten consecutive passes are made, one point is scored. Both offensive groups get the points won to add to their total game scores. For the defense to control the ball and score a point, the two players must pass the ball once between them. This may be done several times in succession, and several points can be scored if the offensive players do not react quickly. Play continues for one minute. At the conclusion of the minute, another group goes on defense, the original defensive group combines with the remaining offensive group, and the process is repeated. Finally, the remaining group goes on defense and the game is completed. The team with the greater number of total points accumulated on both offense and defense is the winner.

Variation: • The size of the playing area can be changed.
• The length of time played can change.

66 – KEEP HEAD UP

DRIBBLING	Center Circle	6 or more Players	1 Ball per Player

Formation: Each player has a ball and is in the center circle.

X—Field Player
Dribble ∿∿⟩
Ball •

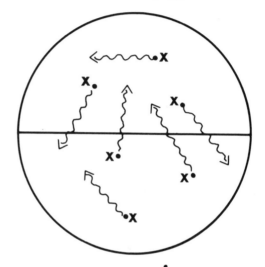

Procedure: All players continue dribbling for a pre-set time period. If a dribbler or his ball touches another player or ball, a point is scored against him. The player with the most points loses.

67 – KEEP IT UP

JUGGLING	Any Area	2 or more Players	1 Ball per Player

Formation: Each player stands with a ball at his feet.

Procedure: Each juggler is allowed two minutes of juggling. A point is scored for each successful juggle and a point is deducted each time the ball hits the ground. The winner is the player with the most points after each round or series of rounds.

Variation: • Organize teams of two to four players each.

68

KICKING FOR DISTANCE

| KICKING | Full Field | 8 or more Players | 4 Balls |

Formation: Four players from each team are lined up along their goal line. Two players on each team have a ball.

X—Field Player
Ball **.**

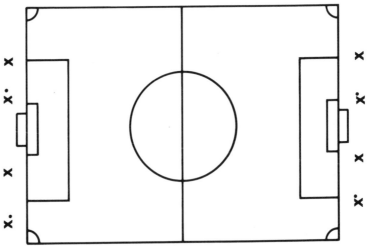

Procedure: The object is to kick the balls over the opponent's goal line. The teams alternate kicks. Each ball is kicked from where it lands. Play continues until one team has kicked three balls over the opposing goal line. If each team kicks two balls over, play starts over again.

69

KICK THE CONES

PASSING	Center Circle	12 Players	6 Balls
			16 Cones

Formation: Two teams of six players each spread out around the center circle. Each player should have a partner directly opposite him, and each pair has one ball. Sixteen cones are placed anywhere in the circle.

X—Field Player
Ball **.**
Cone⊙

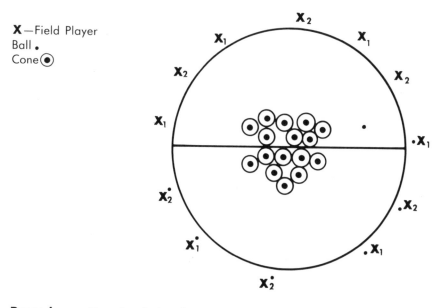

Procedure: At a signal, the players start kicking the balls at the cones and continue kicking until all the cones are knocked down. The team knocking the last cone down wins.

Variation: • Instep kicking only.
• Right or left foot only.

70

KICK THEM OUT

DRIBBLING   Center Circle   2 or more Players   1 Ball per Player
Shielding

Formation: Two teams of equal numbers are in the center circle. Each player has a ball.

X—Field Player
Dribble ⌇⟶
Ball •

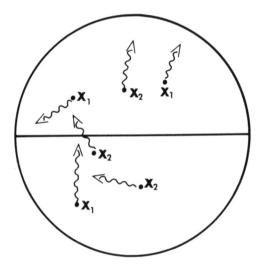

Procedure: On a signal, all players dribble within the center circle. While dribbling, the players on each team try to kick their opponents' balls out of the circle. The team that kicks all the opponents' balls out wins.

Variation: • Play individually. The last man in the circle with a ball wins.

71

KNOCKOUT SOCCER

DRIBBLING   Penalty Area   Groups of 3 Players   1 Ball
                                                                 per Player

Shielding

Contributor: *William A. Seal, III, McDonogh School, McDonogh , Maryland 21208*

Formation: Players form groups of three in the penalty area. Each player has a ball. One player is designated as the dribbler.

X—Field Player
Dribble ⟿
Ball .

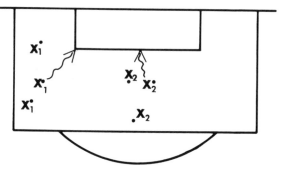

Procedure: The player designated dribbler dribbles and shields his ball. The other two players in the group attempt to knock the dribbler's ball away by passing their ball into the dribblers. The passer may only pass his own ball at the dribbler's ball. When the passer is successful, he scores a point and becomes the dribbler. The first player in the group to score five points is the winner.

72

LINE SOCCER

OFFENSIVE AND DEFENSIVE TECHNIQUES	Penalty Area	16 Players	1 Ball
			4 Cones

Formation: There are two teams of eight players each. Six players from each team spread out along opposite sidelines. Two players from each team are in the center of the area with a ball. A goal marked by two cones five feet apart is on each end line.

X—Field Player
Ball **.**
Cone ◉

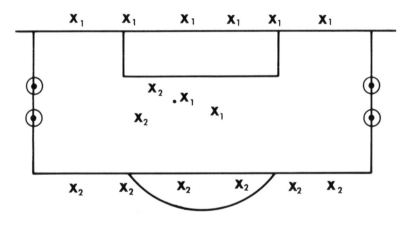

Procedure: The players in the area compete in a two vs. two game for one minute or until a goal is scored by kicking the ball on the ground between the cones. The players on the sidelines may be used, but may only make one touch passes to the players in the area. After time expires or a goal is scored, two new players from each team compete. This rotation continues for a set time period or until a set number of goals are scored.

73

LONG RANGE SOCCER

SHOOTING	Full Field	2 Full Teams	1 Ball
			2 Goals

Offensive and Defensive
Techniques

Formation: Two full teams set up as in a regulation soccer match.

G—Goalkeeper
X—Fieldkeeper
Ball ●

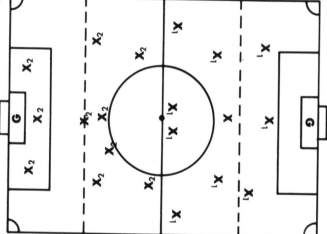

Procedure: This is a regulation soccer game except that all goals must be scored from outside the penalty area. Three points are awarded for a goal. The shooting team scores one point each time the goalkeeper is forced to make a serve. Five points are awarded for each goal scored from outside a line twenty-five yards from goal.

74

LONG SHOTS

SHOOTING	40 yd. by 40 yd. Area	8 Players	1 Ball
		2 Goalkeepers	2 Goals
Passing			

Formation: Two teams of four players are positioned within a different half of the area. One player has a ball. There are two goals, each with a goalkeeper. A line divides the area in half.

G—Goalkeeper
X—Fieldkeeper
Pass — — — —▷
Shot ••••••••••▷
Ball •

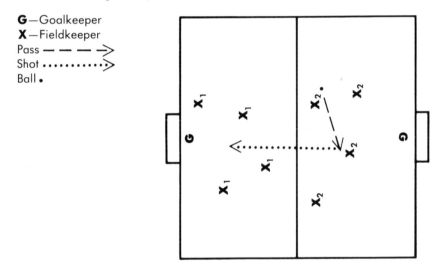

Procedure: This is a five vs. five game, but each team must stay in its own half and must set up to take long shots at the opponent's goal. Players use one or two touch. The team with the most goals after a set time period wins.

75

MAN TO MAN

MARKING   ½ Field   16 to 22 Players   1 Ball

Scrimmage Vests

Contributor: *Tom Griffith, Dartmouth College, Hanover, New Hampshire 03755*

Formation: Two teams of equal numbers are in half field. One team wears scrimmage vests. One player from each team is in the penalty area and the center circle. A field player on one team has a soccer ball.

X—Fieldkeeper
Ball.
Cone ⊙

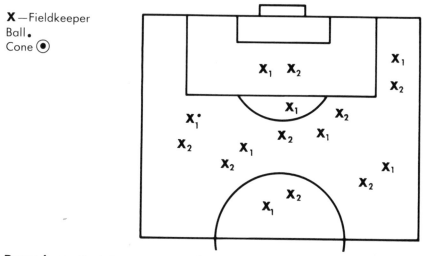

Procedure: Each team can score by getting the ball into the hands of their teammate in either the penalty area or center circle. The opposing players in these areas try to prevent passes to the other players. The players on each team are given an opponent to mark. Otherwise, regulation soccer is played. When a player in the penalty area or center circle catches the ball, his team earns a point. The player with the ball now distributes it to a teammate and play continues. The first team to score ten points wins.

76

MAN UP, MAN DOWN

PASSING	30 yd. by 20 yd. Area	5 Players	1 Ball
			4 Cones

Dribbling

Contributor: *Gary Parsons, Oakland University, Rochester, Michigan 48063*

Formation: Two teams of two players each face each other in the area. One player has a soccer ball. A free player, X_3, is also in the area. Goals are marked by cones four feet apart.

X—Field Player
Ball•
Cone ◉

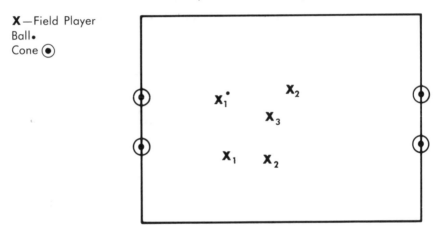

Procedure: This is a three vs. two game. The free player always plays with the team which has possession of the ball. The team scoring the most goals in a set time period wins.

Variation: • Play two vs. one, four vs. three, five vs. four, etc. Vary field size accordingly.

77

MULTIPLE GOAL

OFFENSIVE AND DEFENSIVE TECHNIQUES	Center Circle	2 Players	6 Balls
			12 Cones

Contributor: Jay Martin, Ohio Wesleyan University, Delaware, Ohio 43015

Formation: Two opposing players are in the middle of the center circle. Six goals, marked by cones three feet apart, are spread around the circle. A coach, with a supply of balls, stands just outside the circle.

C —Coach
X —Field Player
Pass — — — ⟶
Sprint ————⟹
Ball •
Cone ⊙

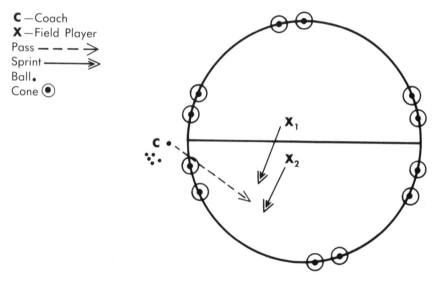

Procedure: This is a one vs. one game which starts when the coach rolls out the ball. The player with the ball tries to score in any goal. As soon as a goal is scored or the ball goes out of the circle, the coach starts play again with a pass. A time limit or specified number of goals determines the winner.

78

NEVER QUIT

DEFENSIVE TECHNIQUES Fitness Goalkeeping	Penalty Area	1 Player a time	6 Balls

Formation: A feeder with a supply of balls faces a field player or goal-keeper.

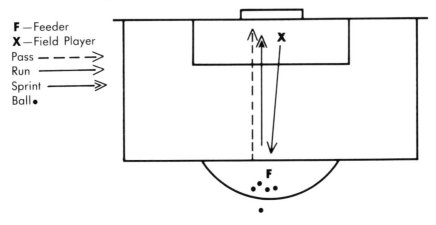

F —Feeder
X —Field Player
Pass — — — ⟶
Run ⟶
Sprint ⟶
Ball •

Procedure: X runs up and taps with his hand the ball held by the feeder. After tapping the ball, the player sprints to the goal. As the player is recovering, the feeder shoots at goal. Field players attempt to save the ball legally while goalkeepers have the advantage of using their hands. The drill continues until the player has attempted ten saves or until a pre-determined time has elapsed (one or two minutes). The winner is the player making the most saves.

79

NO MAN'S LAND

PASSING	Penalty Area	8 Players	1 Ball
			4 Cones

Contributor: *Don A. Scarborough, Brevard College, Brevard, North Carolina 28712*

Formation: Four cones mark an eight yard wide "no man's land" in the center of the penalty area. Three offensive players and one defender are within the area on each side of the "no man's land." An offensive player in one area has a soccer ball.

D — Defensive Player
O — Offensive Player
Cone ⊙
Ball •

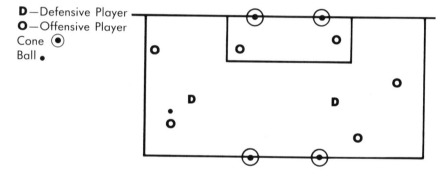

Procedure: The offensive players interpass within their area while the defender pressurizes the man with the ball. The ball is passed in the air across the "no man's land" at the first opportunity. No one may leave his area.

The offensive players try to make as many passes as possible or maintain ball control as long as possible. The defensive player changes places with the offensive player whose pass he intercepts, and the new group continues the game.

80

NO NET VOLLEYBALL

CONTROL   Center Circle   16 to 22 Players   1 Ball

Heading
Kicking

Contributor: *Charles Matlack, Earlham College, Richmond, Indiana 47374*

Formation: Two teams of equal numbers arrange themselves on each side of the center circle's center line. A player on one team stands outside the circle with a ball.

X—Field Player
Pass — — — →
Ball •

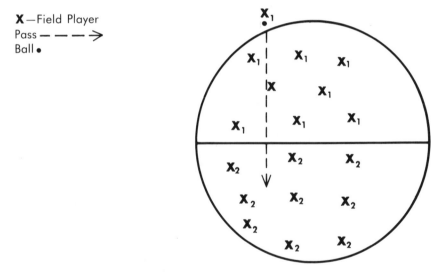

Procedure: The rules of volleyball are followed except that: 1) hands may not be used except to drop the ball to the ground on service, 2) no net is used, 3) the center line divides the area, and 4) the ball may bounce once before being played on each side of the line.

81

NUMBERED WARM-UP

PASSING	¼ to ½ Field	8 or more Players	2 Balls

Contributor: Dr. Thomas R. Martin, West Virginia Wesleyan College, Buckannon, West Virginia 26201

Formation: Players are divided into groups of eight to ten players and spread out within the area. The players wear sequentially numbered vests or shirts. X_1 has a ball.

X—Field Player
Pass — — — ⟶
Ball •

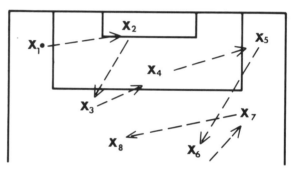

Procedure: The players jog within the area and pass the ball to the next numbered player (i.e. 1 to 2 to 3 and so on). The next player controls and passes the ball on. The highest numbered player passes to No. 1 who starts over. After a few minutes, a second ball is added so that players are constantly looking for the balls, players to pass to, and open space.

Variation: • Restrictions may be added to emphasize specific aspects of play (e.g. one or two touch, chips, etc.)
• The speed of play can be increased.

82

NUTS AND SQUIRRELS

GOALKEEPING   Center Circle   18 to 24 Players   1 Ball
                                                                 per Player
                                          Goalkeeper
Dribbling

Contributor: *Donald L. Lyle, Grove City College, Grove City, Pennsylvania 16127*

Formation: Field players, each with a ball, are within the center circle. One goalkeeper is also in the circle.

G—Goalkeeper
X—Field Player
Dribble
Ball

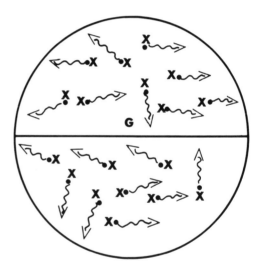

Procedure: At a signal, players dribble within the circle. The goalkeeper isolates one player at a time and attempts to dispossess him of the ball. Time is kept to determine how long each goalkeeper takes to collect a specified number of balls.

Variation: • Use more than one goalkeeper competing against each other to determine who can collect the most balls.

83

ONE IN EIGHT KEEP AWAY

DRIBBLING	½ Field	16 Players	1 Ball

Marking

Contributor: Michael Coven, Brandeis University, Waltham, Massachusetts 02254

Formation: Two teams of eight players each are within half field. A player on one team has a ball.

X—Field Player
Ball •

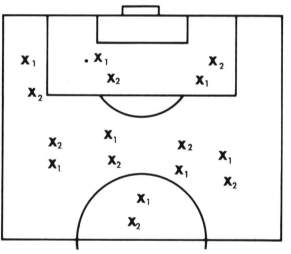

Procedure: Each player has a specific opponent to mark. The player with the ball tries to keep it for one minute by dribbling, feinting, shielding, etc. Only the player assigned to mark the man with the ball may take it away from him. Holding the ball for one minute scores one point. The ball may be passed off, but no point is scored if it is passed off in less than a minute. The first team to score five points wins.

84 – ONE ON ONE

OFFENSIVE AND ½ Field	12 or more Players 3 Balls
DEFENSIVE	
TECHNIQUES	Goalkeeper Goal

Formation: Six defensemen line up behind one post of the goal. Six or more offensive players line up at the center circle. A goalkeeper is in goal.

D—Defensive Player
G—Goalkeeper
O—Offensive Player
Dribble ∿∿∿⇒
Pass – – – – – ⇒
Run ⎯⎯⎯⇒
Shot ••••••••••⇒
Ball •

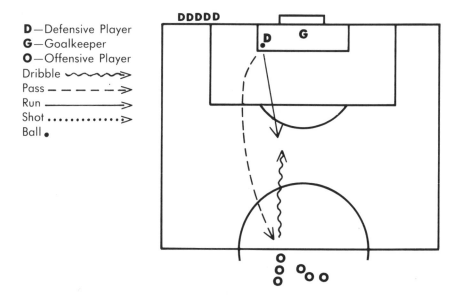

Procedure: A defensive player kicks a goalkick to the center circle. The waiting offensive player receives the ball and dribbles toward the goal. The defensive player who took the goal-kick runs to meet the offensive player and attempts to tackle. If the defensive player is successful, the play ends, and the offensive and defensive players go to the end of their respective lines. If the forward is able to maintain possession to the edge of the penalty area, the defensive player releases and the goalkeeper plays the forward one on one. The offense scores five points for each goal, and the defense scores one point each time an attacker fails to score. The group with the most points after a set time or number of attempts wins.

85

ONE OUT SOCCER BASEBALL

CONTROL	½ Field	12 to 22 Players	1 Ball
			1 Goal
Fitness			2 Cones

Contributor: Alan A. Goodyear, Rensselaer Polytechnic Institute, Troy, New York, 12144

Formation: One team of six players is spread out in half field. The team "at bat" stands outside the center circle. A feeder (pitcher) stands fifteen yards from home plate which is marked by a cone at the midpoint of the circle. First base is marked by a cone at the midpoint of the eighteen yard line.

D—Defensive Player
F—Feeder
O—Offensive Player
Pass — — — —>
Ball •
Cone ⊙

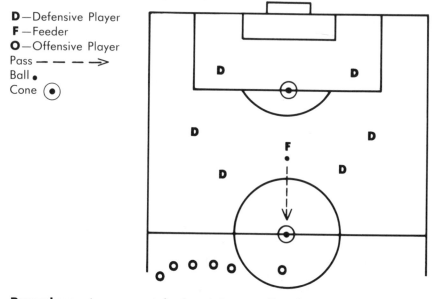

Procedure: A permanent feeder pitches a rolling ball to the batter in the center circle. Each batter has only one pitch to kick and each team gets only one "out" per inning. After kicking the ball, the batter must reach first base before being put out. The batter may also try to reach home on his kick. The player on first base must reach home on the next kick before an out is made.

An out is made by; 1) the batter missing the ball, failing to kick it out of the center circle, or kicking it behind him; 2) the fielders hitting the base or runner with the ball before he reaches first or home; 3) the fielders "catching" a fly ball by controlling the ball with five consecutive touches without the ball hitting the ground. An automatic home run is scored when the ball is kicked in the goal. Whoever first gets a specified number of runs, or is ahead after a specified number of innings, is the winner.

86

ONE vs ONE

SHOOTING   20 yd. by 10 yd. Area   2 or more Players   1 Ball
                                                              Kickboard

Formation: Two players, one with a ball, stand about twenty yards from a kickboard. A regulation goal is marked on the board.

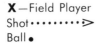

X—Field Player
Shot · · · · · · · · ▷
Ball •

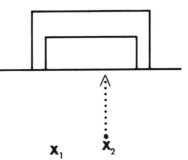

Procedure: X₁ starts the game with a free kick on goal. Each player takes alternate shots on goal until one player misses the ball or goal for which the player not missing the ball or goal earns a point. The first player to score five points wins.

Variation: • Play two vs. two.
                  • With more players, play one vs. one or two vs. two with the winner staying on.

87

OUT

SHOOTING	Penalty Area	2 or more Players	1 Ball per Player

Formation: Each player, with a ball, stands on the eighteen yard line.

X—Field Player
Shot ·········>
Ball •

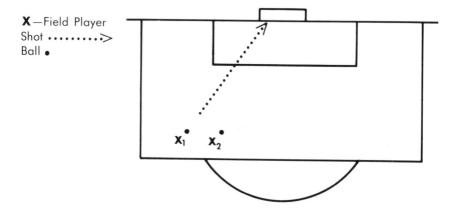

Procedure: The players toss a coin or choose the order of shooting. The first player may stand anywhere along the eighteen yard line. He must announce where on goal he is attempting to shoot and what foot he will use. If, in the coach's judgement, the attempt is good, the next player must do the same shot successfully. If he fails, he gets a letter (i.e. "O"). If he is successful, the next player goes under the same conditions and so on until someone misses. After a miss, the next player has a free choice shot. A player who gets three letters is "OUT." The last player remaining wins.

88

OUTMANNED

OFFENSIVE AND ½ Field DEFENSIVE TECHNIQUES	8 Players	1 Ball
	Goalkeeper	

Formation: Six offensive players and three defensive players, one of whom is a goalkeeper, occupy one half of a field or a more confined area.

D—Defensive Player
O—Offensive Player
Ball •

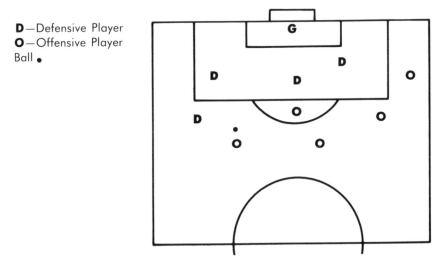

Procedure: The six offensive players exploit the advantage and attempt to score as many goals as possible in a given time period. The offense receives one point for each goal. The defense receives one point for each completed pass and two points for each pass over midfield that is on the ground. The team scoring the greater number of points within a prescribed time period wins.

89

PARALLEL ZONE SOCCER

PASSING	Full Field	16 Players	1 Ball

Formation: Two teams of eight players each (X_1 and X_2) are split into groups of four. The groups occupy alternate zones. One team, X_1, has a ball.

X—Field Player
Pass — — —$\rightarrow$
Ball •

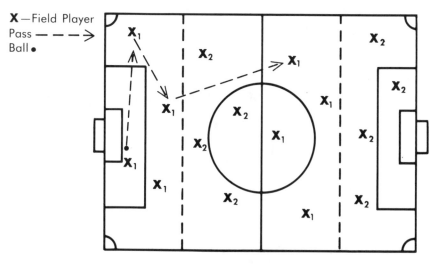

Procedure: The X_1 players interpass within and between their zones. The X_2 players try to intercept the cross zone passes and then pass within and between their zones. The ball may not be passed more than three times nor dribbled within one zone.

90

PASSING CONCENTRATION

PASSING	Penalty Area	10 Players	2 Balls
			10 Vests
Receiving			

Formation: Ten players form two teams and are positioned in the penalty area. Each team has one ball and wears different colored vests.

X—Field Player
Pass — — —⟩
Ball .

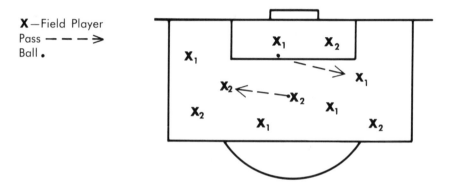

Procedure: Each team passes among themselves and keeps track of the number of consecutive passes. Players on the opposing team do not attempt to intercept passes; however, the area is congested and part of the challenge is to avoid hitting players. The team making the most consecutive passes in a specified time period is the winner.

91

PASSING SOCCER

PASSING	½ Field	12 Players	1 Ball

Formation: Two teams of six players each are spread throughout half-field. A player on one team has a soccer ball.

X —Field Player
Pass — — —➤
Ball •

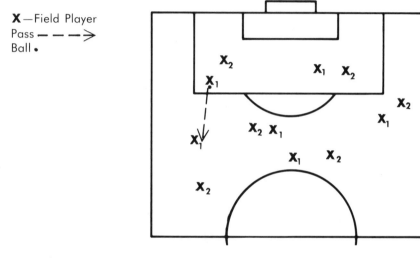

Procedure: A team must make five or more consecutive passes to score a point. All passes must be made with the inside of the foot.

Variation: • Put a one or two touch restriction on passes.

92

PASS IT THROUGH

PASSING	10 yd. by 5 yd. Area	4 or more Players	1 Ball per Team
			2 Cones per Team

Formation: Teams of two to four players stand about five yards apart on both sides of a one yard goal marked by cones.

X—Field Player
Pass – – –$\rightarrow$
Ball •
Cone ⊙

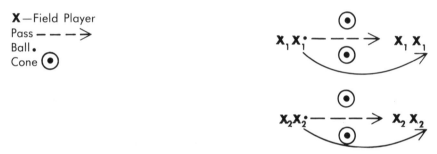

Procedure: On a signal, the players on each team take turns passing the ball through the goal to a teammate, using only an inside pass. After each pass, the player making the pass goes to the end of the opposite line. A point is scored each time the ball passes through the goal. The game lasts for three minutes.

Variation: • Use right or left foot only.
• Alternate feet.
• Increase the distance from the goal.
• Use one or two touch passing.

93

PASS OR HIT THE CONE

PASSING	½ Field	10 to 16 Players	1 Ball
Marking			2 Cones

Contributor: *Art Rikstad, North Plainfield High School, North Plainfield, New Jersey 07062*

Formation: Two teams of equal numbers are spread out in half field. One team has the soccer ball. One cone is located at the mid-point of each sideline.

X—Field Player
Ball **.**
Cone **⊙**

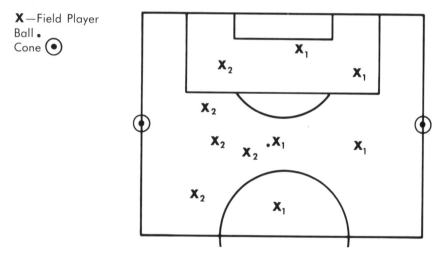

Procedure: The team in possession may score a point by hitting the opponents' cone or by completing ten consecutive passes. If a team loses possession of the ball, the passes completed are wiped out as soon as the team in possession completes one pass. If they regain possession before the opponent can complete one pass, the count continues from the original number. The first team to score five points wins.

Variation:
- Play one or two touch.
- Require all passes to be at least ten yards.

94

PENALTY KICK COMPETITION

PENALTY KICKING	Penalty Area	1 Player	1 Ball
Goalkeeping		Goalkeeper	Goal

Formation: A player is at the penalty mark and a goalkeeper is in goal.

G—Goalkeeper
X—Field Player
Ball •

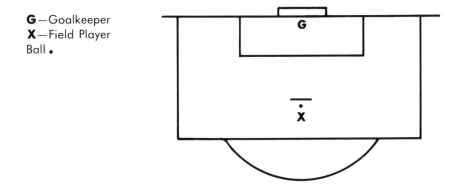

Procedure: The field player takes twelve penalty kicks. Score is kept. The kicker receives one point each time he scores, and the goalkeeper receives one point each time he makes a save. In addition, a point is deducted from the kicker's score each time he misses the goal.

Variation: • Competitions can be set up in other ways, e.g.:
    a. One vs. one with each player taking five shots.
    b. Five vs. five with each player taking one shot.
    c. The full team participating with a player eliminated if he misses the goal or the goalie makes the save. Competition continues until one player remains.
    • Change goalkeepers after every five shots or after every shot.

95

PENETRATION SOCCER

OFFENSIVE AND ½ Field DEFENSIVE TECHNIQUES Shooting	10 Players 2 Goalkeepers	1 Ball 2 Small Goals

Formation: Two teams of five players and one goalkeeper each line up in a half field. A small goal, of indoor size, is placed at the midpint of each sideline. One team has a soccer ball. Two cones are appropriately placed to mark an imaginary center line.

G—Goalkeeper
X—Field Player
Ball •
Cone ⊙

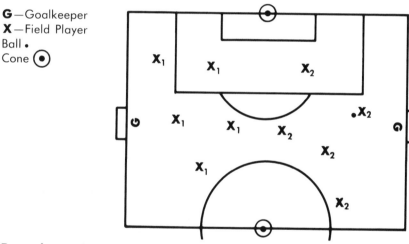

Procedure: This is a five vs. five game played in a half-field using the sidelines as endlines. Each team has a goalkeeper who cannot use his hands.

Points are scored as follows:
- One point for each pass made by a team from its defensive half of the area across the center line to an attacker who has beaten the last opposing defender.
- One point for every shot on goal deflected by the keeper.
- Three points for a goal.

The team accumulating the most points in a set time period is the winner.

96

POSSESSION

| CONTROL | ½ or Full Field | 12 to 18 Players | 1 Ball |

Contributor: Bud Lewis, Wilmington College, Wilmington, Ohio 45177

Formation: The playing field is divided into thirds. There are three offensive players and two defenders in both rectangle A and rectangle C. In rectangle B, there is a one vs. one set up.

D—Defensive Player
O—Offensive Player
Ball •

Procedure: Play begins in rectangle A. O_1, O_2 and O_3 try to maintain possession within the area. D_1 and D_2 attempt to win the ball, and when successful, clear the ball to D_3 in rectangle B. D_3 tries to beat O_4 and get the ball to D_4, D_5 and D_6 in rectangle C, while O_4 tries to intercept the ball and return it to his teammates in rectangle A. Play continues back and forth in this manner for a specified time period or number of points are scored. One point is awarded each time the ball moves from rectangle A to C by team D or vice versa by team O.

Variation:
• Increase the number of players in each area.
• Put a second ball in play.

97

PRESSURE COOKER

OFFENSIVE AND   40 yd. by 20 yd. Area   10 Players   1 Ball
DEFENSIVE
TECHNIQUES

Passing

Formation: Five offensive players and five defensive players are in the area. One of the defenders stands just outside the area. The attackers have the ball.

O—Offensive Player
D—Defensive Player
Ball •

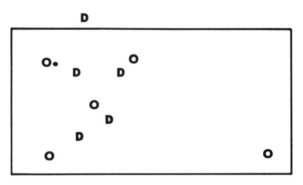

Procedure: Five attackers play against four defenders and attempt to make as many passes as possible in a three minute period. A fifth defender stands outside the area and counts the passes, interceptions, tackles or out of bounds kicks. One of the attackers stays away from the action so that the other attackers can play a long ball to him. After three minutes, the roles are reversed. The team with the most passes wins.

98

PROTECT AND DEFLECT

SHIELDING   Center Circle   20 to 30 Players   15 Balls

Dribbling

Contributor: *John Boles, Temple University, Philadephia, Pennsylvania 19122*

Formation: The team is divided into two groups of equal numbers. One group spreads out around the center circle. The other group spreads out within the circle. Each player in the circle has a soccer ball.

X—Field Player
Dribble 〰⟫
Ball •

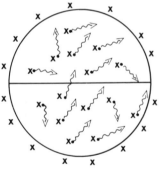

Procedure: The game consists of three parts. During the first part, the players in the circle continue dribbling with heads up, using sides of feet only, while changing pace and direction. After thirty seconds, the two groups change and the outside players become dribblers while the original dribblers rest. During the second part, the players within the circle dribble forward, backwards and sidewards, using only the soles of the feet. The groups change again after thirty seconds. In the third part, each player in the circle shields and protects his ball while trying to deflect the other players' balls. A player who loses control of his ball or has it deflected is out of the game. Teams change when one player remains. The last player in each group is the winner.

Variation: • Make the dribbling area smaller by using only half or one quarter of the circle.

99

PROTECTION

OFFENSIVE AND DEFENSIVE TECHNIQUES	7 yd. to 10 yd. Radius Circle	6 to 8 Players	1 Ball 1 Cone per Player

Contributor: Owen L. Wright, Elizabethtown College, Elizabethtown, Pennsylvania 17022

Formation: Cones are placed in a circle with each player protecting a cone. A ball is in the center of the area.

X—Field Player
Ball **.**
Cone ◉

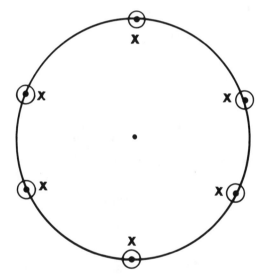

Procedure: The object of the game is to try to hit the other players' cones and, at the same time, protect your cone from being hit. One point is scored for hitting an opponent's cones, and the player whose cone is hit gets a minus point. Each player must protect his own cone; however, in order to score he must take the risk of leaving his cone. A ball played out of bounds is put back in the middle for anyone to play. After a score, the player scored against starts play immediately. A minus three or plus three score may be used to end the game.

100

QUICK DRAW

| OFFENSIVE TECHNIQUES | Any Area | 2 or more Players | 1 Ball per pair |

Contributor: *Armand Dikranian, Southern Connecticut State College, New Haven, Connecticut 06515*

Formation: Two players stand one yard apart from each other with a ball midway between them.

X—Field Player   **X • X**
Ball •

Procedure: On a command, each player tries to beat his opponent by drawing the ball to him. Play the best of seven tries.

Variation:
- Use any foot.
- Use only the left or right foot.
- Face away from each other, turn and draw.

101

QUICK SHOOTING

SHOOTING	½ Field	12 Players	6 Balls
Fitness		Goalkeeper	

Formation: Offensive players line up at mid-field alongside the feeder. Defensive players form a line at the side of the field at a point eighteen yards from the goal. Two of the defensive players serve as retrievers.

D—Defensive Player
F—Feeder,
G—Goalkeeper
O—Offensive Player
R—Retriever
Dribble ～～～>
Pass – – – – >
Run ———>
Sprint ——>>
Ball ●

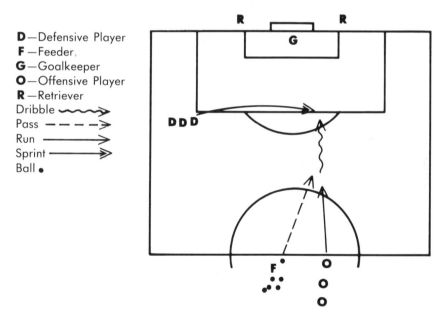

Procedure: The feeder passes the ball forward for the offensive player to dribble and shoot. At a given signal, the defender sprints to confront the offensive player. The object is for the offensive player to get a good shot on goal before being confronted by the defender. Offensive players receive five points for each goal. Defenders receive a point each time a goal is not scored.

102

RACE TO SCORE

OFFENSIVE AND DEFENSIVE TECHNIQUES	Penalty Area	4 or more Players	1 Ball
Passing Shooting			4 Cones

Contributor: *John F. McMullan, Oceanside High School, Oceanside, New York 11572*

Formation: Goals designated by cones two yards apart are at each end of the penalty area. Pairs of players are at the midway point of the penalty area on the goal line and eighteen yard line. A ball is midway between the pairs of players in the center of the penalty area.

X—Field Player
Ball **.**
Cone (●)

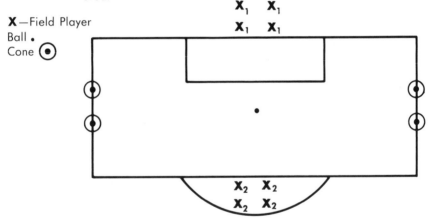

Procedure: At a signal, the first two X₁ players and first X₂ players race to the ball. The team reaching the ball first attempts to score at either goal. The other team plays man to man defense until they gain ball possession and then become offensive players. Before a goal may be scored, both offensive players must touch the ball. Once a shot is taken, the ball is returned to the center and a second signal brings on the next two pairs of players. The first team scoring ten goals wins.

Variation: • Play one vs. one, three vs. three, or four vs. four.

103

RECEIVE AND SHOOT

SHOOTING   30 yd. by 20 yd. Area   2 Players   10 Balls

                                    2 Goalkeepers 2 Goals

Defensive Techniques

Formation: Two field players stand in the middle of the playing area facing each other and a goal. A feeder serves a ball between them. Goalkeepers are in each goal.

F —Feeder
G —Goalkeeper
X —Field Player
Pass — — — ⟹
Ball •

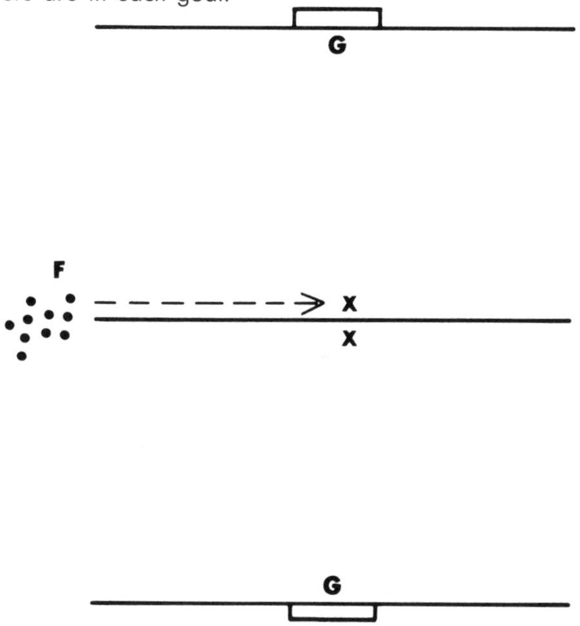

Procedure: The feeder serves the ball between the two players. The player gaining control immediately shoots at the goal he is facing. The other player defends against the shot. As soon as one ball is used, i.e., goes out of play, another ball is served. The first player to score a goal is the winner.

Variation: • Assign two players to each team and permit a pass before the shot.

104

RUN AND THROW

THROWING	Full Field	20 Players	1 Ball
		2 Goalkeepers	

Formation: Two full teams are positioned as in a regulation game.

G—Goalkeeper
X—Field Player
Ball ●

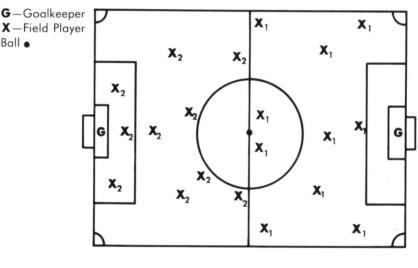

Procedure: The only way to pass or score is by a throw-in. A foul throw results in the other team getting possession of the ball with a free throw-in from the point of infraction. The ball may also be advanced by dribbling, soccer style or basketball style. Since passing is restricted to throw-ins, players may catch the ball to receive a pass. Shots on goal are throw-ins into the net.

105

SARDINES

PASSING	Center Circle	12 to 24 Players	4 Balls
			Scrimmage Vests

Contributor: *George R. Logan, San Diego State University, San Diego, California 92182*

Formation: Four squads of three to six players each are located within the center circle or similar size area. Each squad wears different colored vests and has one ball, which should be a different color than the others.

B —Player With Blue Vest
G —Player With Green Vest
R —Player With Red Vest
Y —Player With Yellow Vest
Ball •

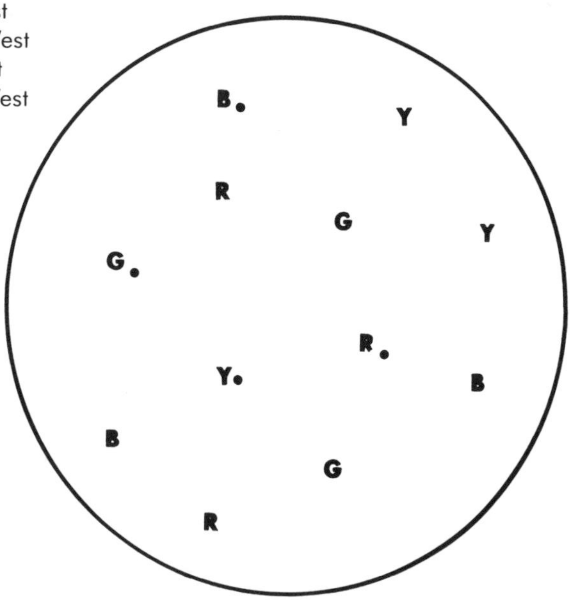

Procedure: The players interpass among their own squad. The team completing the greatest number of passes in a set time period wins.

Variation: • Introduce restrictions, e.g., one touch, two touch, left foot only, etc.

106

SCORING FOR FUN

OFFENSIVE AND DEFENSIVE TECHNIQUES	½ Field	10 Players	Several Balls
		Goalkeeper	

Contributor: *Fran Bacon, University of Bridgeport, Bridgeport, Connecticut 06602*

Formation: Six offensive players and four defensive players are in one half of the soccer field. A goalkeeper defends the regulation goal. Two cones, twenty-four feet apart at mid-field, serve as a goal. One offensive player has a soccer ball.

D—Defensive Player
G—Goalkeeper
O—Offensive Player
Ball •
Cone ⊙

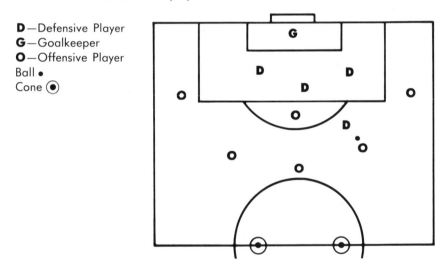

Procedure: Six offensive players play against four defenders and a goal-keeper. The ball is put into play by the offense. The offensive team tries to score in the regulation goal, while the defensive team tries to score by kicking the ball on the ground through the cones. One point is awarded for a goal by the offense and two points for a goal by the defense. The first team to score six points wins.

107

SECOND CHOICE PASSING

MOVING WITHOUT THE BALL Passing Shooting	½ Field	12 Players	1 Ball 2 Goals

Contributor: Kenneth Kutler, Frostburg State College, Frostburg, Maryland 21532

Formation: Two teams of six players each are within a half field area. Two small goals or cones are placed on opposite sidelines. One team has a soccer ball.

X—Field Player
Pass — — — ⟩
Run ——————⟩
Shot ·········⟩
Ball •

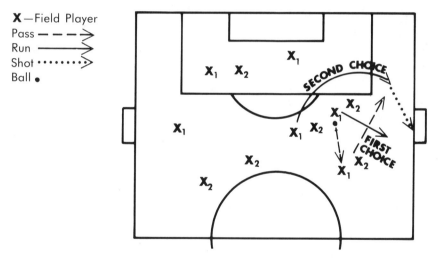

Procedure: This is a six vs. six game with the restriction that each time a team has possession of the balls, it can shoot for the goal only after at least one "second choice" pass is made. (See diagram for example.)

Variation: • Use hands instead of feet.
• Goals are scored by heading.

108

SHOOTING UNDER PRESSURE

SHOOTING	Penalty Area	12 Players	10 Balls
			2 Goals

Contributor: *Pat McStay, Neptune High School, Neptune, New Jersey 07753*

Formation: There are two teams of six players each. Three players from each team are within the penalty area with the other players in their respective goal. A feeder with ten balls is outside the penalty area.

F —Feeder
X —Field Player
Pass — — — ⟩
Shot ⋯⋯⋯⟩
Ball •

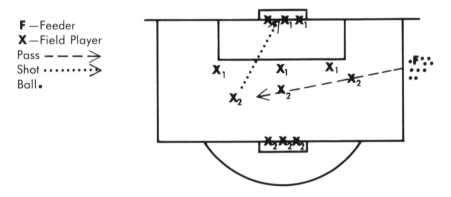

Procedure: The feeder serves a ball into the area, and the two teams compete with each other to get a shot on goal as soon as possible. The feeder continues to serve balls as soon as a ball is shot into the goal or goes out of bounds. The players in the goal can act as goalkeepers but may not use their hands. After ten balls are served, the field players and the players in the goal switch positions. The team scoring the most goals after twenty balls wins.

Variation: • Shots must be taken before a specified maximum of passes.
• Add goalkeepers.
• Forbid dribbling.

109

SHOOT OUT

SHOOTING	½ Field	10 Players	1 Ball per Offensive Player
Receiving		Goalkeeper	

Contributor: *Richard J. Daoust, John F. Kennedy High School, Bellmore, New York 11710*

Formation: Five offensive players, each with a ball, are in the center circle. Five defensive players line up on the goal line. A goalkeeper is in goal.

D—Defensive Player
G—Goalkeeper
O—Offensive Player
Ball •
Dribble ∿∿⟩
Shot •••••••⟩

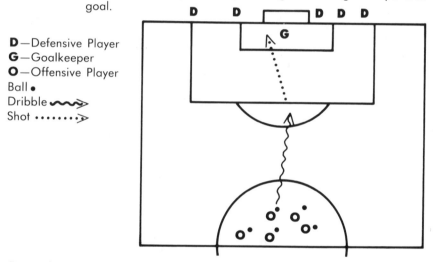

Procedure: Offensive players, in order, dribble to the edge of the penalty area. At this point, the offensive player must shoot on goal. If he scores, his team is awarded one point. The goalkeeper attempts to make the save and, if successful, no points are scored. If the ball goes wide or over the goal, defensive players attempt to receive the ball cleanly, and if successful, a point is scored by the defensive team. After all five offensive players have taken shots, offensive and defensive roles change. The team scoring the most points wins.

Variation:
• Vary the type of shot (instep, inside of foot, non-dominant foot).
• Vary the distance from which the shot may be taken.

110

SHOOT THE BALL

SHOOTING	½ Field	14 Players	6 Balls
			1 Goal
Passing			

Formation: Seven attackers and seven defenders are within half-field. The attackers have a ball. A supply of balls is available at midfield.

D—Defensive Player
O—Offensive Player
Pass — — — →
Shot ••••••••••>
Ball •

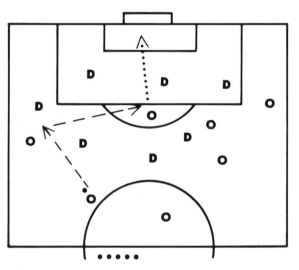

Procedure: Seven attackers have five minutes to score as many goals as possible. After five minutes, the defenders have a chance to attack. The team scoring the most goals wins.

Variation: • Count shots on goal.
• Add a goalkeeper.

111

SHOOT WITH OPPOSITION

SHOOTING	Penalty Area	8 to 24 Players	10 Balls
Defensive Techniques		1 to 3 Goalkeepers	

Formation: Defensive players form two lines, one behind each goalpost. Offensive players form two lines at the outer corners of the penalty area. A goalkeeper is in the goal. Five balls are off the field of play by each post.

D —Defensive Player
O —Offensive Player
G —Goalkeeper
Pass — — — ⟶
Run ⟶
Dribble ⟶
Shot ·········⟶
Ball •

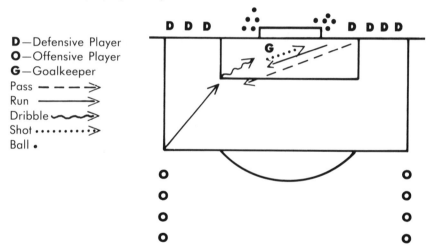

Procedure: The first man in one of the defensive lines passes the ball to the first offensive player in the diagonally opposite line. The defensive player then runs to defend against the offensive player who attempts to score. After the play, the defensive player goes to the end of the other defensive line, and the offensive player goes to the end of the other offensive line. The offense gets five points for each goal, and the defense gets one point each time a goal is not scored.

Variation: • A feeder serves high balls to offensive players to be headed on goal.

112

SHOTS GALORE

SHOOTING   50 yd. by 50 yd. Area   12 Players   1 Ball

                                          2 Goalkeepers   4 Cones

Goalkeeping
Offensive and Defensive   Vests
Techniques

Formation: Four cones designate four goals in the center of the area. Each goal is regulation width. Two goalkeepers defend the four goals. Two teams (in different colored vests) of six players each are positioned in the area in front of one of the goals. One team is on offense, and the other on defense.

D—Defensive Player
O—Offensive Player
G—Goalkeeper
Ball •
Cone ⊙

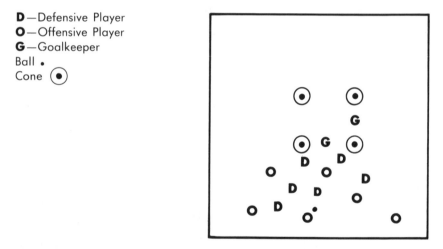

Procedure: The offensive team attempts to score goals. Shots may be taken at any of the four goals. Defenders attempt to prevent goals and goalkeepers protect all four goals. Obviously, the goal at the point of attack is always defended. After five minutes of play, the offense and defense change roles. The team scoring the greatest number of goals in the ten minute period wins.

113

SHOW AND HOLD

RECEIVING	30 yd. by 15 ft. Area	3 Players	1 Ball

Communication   1 Cone
Offensive and Defensive Techniques

Contributor: Leonard Long, Virginia Wesleyan College, Norfolk, Virginia 23502

Formation: A cone serves as a goal. An offensive player and a defensive player stand near the cone. A feeder, with a soccer ball, stands about thirty yards from the players.

D—Defensive Player
F—Feeder
O—Offensive Player
Pass — — — ⟶
Sprint ⟶
Ball •
Cone ⊙

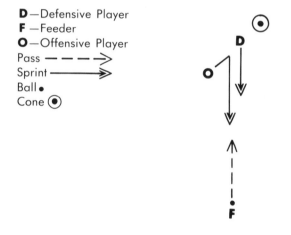

Procedure: O checks toward D, then turns and sprints toward the feeder who passes to him at O_1. The defender stays with the offensive player and applies pressure. Defense should start off as passive and increase to total pressure. O, by communicating with the feeder, will decide to pass back to the feeder or turn and attack. Five points are scored by the offensive player when he makes a successful attack, and one point each time the defender thwarts an attack. The first player to score ten points wins.

114

SHUTTLE DRIBBLE RELAY

DRIBBLING   Any Area   6 or more Players   1 Ball
                                                            per team

                                                            4 Cones
                                                            per team
Fitness

Formation: Teams of three players each line up ten yards from a series of four cones which are in a straight line, five yards apart. The first player in each line has a ball.

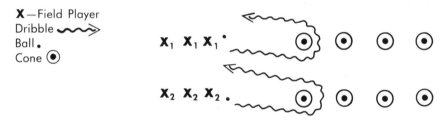

X—Field Player
Dribble 〰️➤
Ball •
Cone ⊙

Procedure: The first player in each line dribbles around the first cone in his line and back to the starting line. Each team member takes a turn going around the first cone. This procedure is followed for each cone.

115

SIEVE

DRIBBLING   40 yd. by 20 yd. Area   14 Players   7 Balls
Tackling

Formation: Seven attackers, each with a ball, line up at one end line of the area. The area is marked off into three ten yard tackling areas alternating with two five yard neutral areas. Three defenders are in the first tackling area, two in the second, and two in the third.

D—Defensive Player
O—Offensive Player
Dribble ~~~>
Ball.

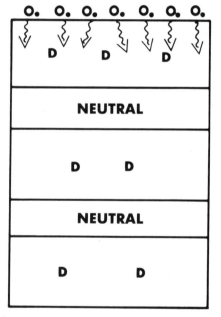

Procedure: On a signal, each attacker tries to dribble through the tackling zones. The team earns one point each time a player is successful in getting through a tackling zone. Defenders must stay within their area. If a ball is lost to a defender, that ball and player are out of the game. After each attacker finishes, the teams change roles and the game is repeated. The team earning the most points wins.

116

SIMON SAYS

DRIBBLING	Center Circle	10 to 20 Players	1 Ball
			for each player

Contributor: *Larry M. Gross, North Carolina State University, Raleigh, North Carolina 27650*

Formation: Each player, in possession of a ball, is in the center circle. The coach is also in the circle.

C —Coach
X —Field Player
Ball

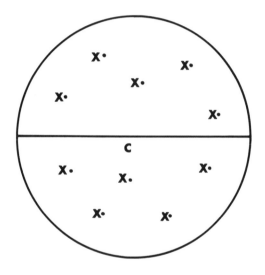

Procedure: Players, while dribbling continually, must react immediately to the coach's commands: For example, "dribble with ouside of right foot," "change direction," "go backward," "stop ball with chest," "place nose on ball," and so on. Although commands are given verbally, the players are to react only when the coach's hand, held in a fist over his head, opens up. This forces players to keep their heads up as well as listen for the commands.

Players making mistakes, reacting late or when the hand is not opened are eliminated and must go outside the circle and juggle the ball. The last player remaining in the circle wins.

117

SLALOM DRIBBLE RELAY

DRIBBLING   Any Area   6 or more Players   1 Ball
per Team

6 Cones
per Team

Formation: Teams of three players line up three yards from the first of a series of six cones, three yards apart, marked off in a zig zag course. The first player in each line has a ball.

X—Field Player
Dribble
Ball .
Cone

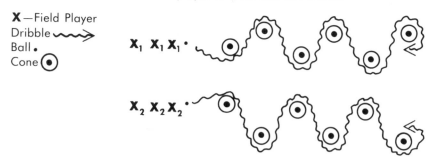

Procedure: Teams of three players compete in a relay race by dribbling through the course. After dribbling around the last cone, each player dribbles in a straight line through the cones and touches the next player in line.

Variation: • Dribble the zig-zag course in both directions.

118

SOCCER BADMINTON

CONTROL   Badminton Court   2 or 4 Players   1 Ball

                                                          Badminton Net

Passing

Formation: A player is in the even (right) service court on one side with a ball. Another player is in the diagonally opposite service court.

X—Field Player
Pass — — — ⟶
Ball●

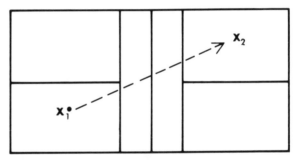

Procedure: X_1 serves a volley kick to X_2. All balls may be returned on the volley or after one bounce. There are unlimited touches per side. If the serve touches the net or goes out of bounds, it is a side out. Each game consists of fifteen points. Points are scored only while serving. A line ball is good. Hands may only be used on the serve.

Variation: • Play doubles.
                • No bounces are allowed.

119

SOCCER BASEBALL

KICKING	Any Large Area	8 to 20 Players	1 Ball
			4 Cones
Passing			

Contributor: *John Fellenbaum, Franklin and Marshall College, Lancaster, Pennsylvania 17607*

Formation: There are two teams of equal numbers. The offensive players are "at bat" and form a line behind home plate. The first player up has a soccer ball. The defensive players take positions in the field similar to baseball. Four cones are used as three bases and home plate.

D—Defensive Player
O—Offensive Player
Pass — — — ⟶
Run ⟶
Shot ....⟶
Ball •
Cone ⊙

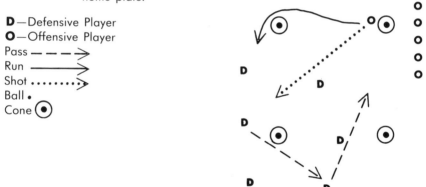

Procedure: The offensive player "at bat" kicks a stationary ball into the playing area. He then attempts to circle the bases before the defensive team, using soccer skills, gets the ball home. A run is scored if the offensive player crosses home plate before the ball. The player is out if the ball reaches home first. Each team "at bat" gets three outs. A set number of innings is played.

Variation: • The player at bat must use a specific foot or make a specific type kick.
• The defensive team must complete a specified number of passes before kicking the ball home.

120

SOCCER DODGEBALL

PASSING	Center Circle	12 or more Players 8 or more Balls
Fitness		

Formation: Eight players, each with a ball, spread around the center circle. Four players are within the circle.

X—Field Player
Ball •

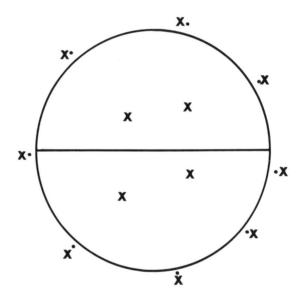

Procedure: The outside players try to hit the middle target players with the balls. As a player is hit, he joins the outside group. See who lasts the longest. When all the target players have been hit, four new players get a chance to be in the target group.

121

SOCCER GOLF

PASSING   Penalty Area   2 or more Players   1 Ball per Player

9 to 18 Cones

Formation: Each player has a ball and stands at a spot five yards from the first cone. Cones or markers are scattered throughout the area.

X—Field Player
Pass — — — →
Ball .
Cone ⊙

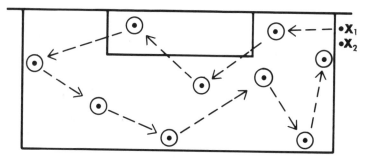

Procedure: Each player has a ball and competes against a paired opponent to see how many passes it takes to travel completely around the couse, using only inside of foot passes. The players alternate passes.
As in golf, the lowest score wins.

Variation: • The player who goes around the course in the fastest time, regardless of the number of passes, is the winner.
• Increase the size of the area.

122

SOCCER HANDBALL

FITNESS   Handball Court   2 to 4 Players   1 Ball

Control

Formation: One player, with a ball, stands in the serving area. The other player stands in the major portion of the court.

X—Field Player
Ball•

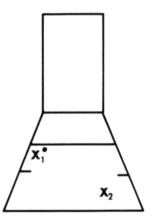

Procedure: This is a handball game using a soccer ball which can be played on a four wall or single wall court. Singles or doubles may be played. The ball is served by a volley or half-volley from the service area. The serve must strike the front wall and land on or beyond the service line. A server is allowed one short or one long serve; two bad serves is a side out.

All balls must be played by any legal soccer skill before or after one bounce and returned to the front wall without striking the floor. Ball control (juggling) is permitted as long as the ball does not touch the floor. A returned ball striking an opponent before hitting the floor or wall is played over. Each game consists of fifteen points. Points are scored only while serving.

123

SOCCER TENNIS

CONTROL	Tennis Court	2 or 4 Players	1 Ball

Tennis Net

Passing

Formation: A player is on each baseline diagonally opposite his opponent. One player has a ball.

X—Field Player
Pass — — —➤
Ball •

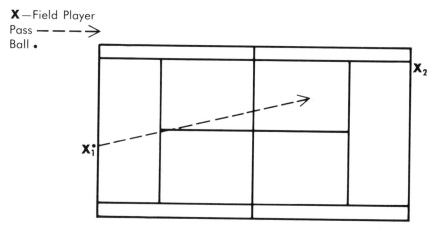

Procedure: This is a singles tennis game, using a soccer ball, and with the following modifications:
- The ball is served from the baseline by a volley or half volley and must land in the proper service court.
- The serve is lost if it hits the net or goes out of bounds.
- The serve must strike the ground before being returned. All other balls may be returned on the volley but before more than one bounce. There are unlimited touches per side.
- A ball hitting the line is good.
- The hands may be used only on the serve.
- A game is fifteen points. Points are scored only when serving.

Variation:
- Play doubles.

124

SOCCER VOLLEYBALL

HEADING	Volleyball Court	6 to 12 Players	1 Ball
			1 Volleyball Net
Control			

Formation: Two teams of equal numbers occupy respective sides of a volleyball court. One team has a ball.

X —Field Player
Ball •

Procedure: Play is begun by a head service from a front line player who throws the ball in the air and heads it over the net. The ball may be kept in play by using any legal part of the body, but the ball must be headed over the net. A game consists of fifteen points. Points are scored only while serving. Teams rotate in a clockwise order when the serve is regained and a new player serves.

125

SPRINT AND HEAD

FITNESS	15 yd. by 15 yd. Area	3 Players	6 Balls
			1 Cone
			1 Goal
Heading			

Formation: One player, X_1, is on a line ten yards from a goal (or wall). A cone is five yards further from the goal. Two other players, X_2 and X_3, are in front of each side of the goal.

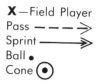

X —Field Player
Pass $- - - \gg$
Sprint $\longrightarrow$
Ball •
Cone ⊙

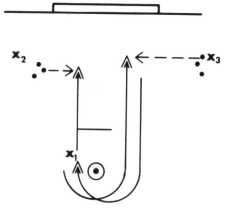

Procedure: On signal, X_1 sprints around the cone and toward the goal where he heads balls thrown alternately by X_2 and X_3. The balls should be thrown so that X_1 does not have to slow down and has to jump to head each ball. One ball is to be headed over the goal and the other into the goal. X_1 continues sprinting and heading for forty-five seconds after which the players change positions. Record the number of balls headed within the time period.

126

SPRINT AND SHOOT

FITNESS	15 yd. by 15 yd. Area	3 Players	3 Balls
			1 Cone
Shooting			1 Small Goal

Formation: Two players, X_1 and X_2, are on a line ten yards from a small goal or wall. A cone is five yards further from the goal. A third player, X_3, stands near the goal.

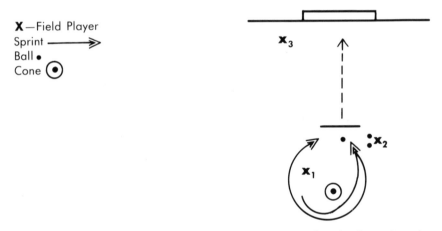

X—Field Player
Sprint ——————⟩
Ball •
Cone ⊙

Procedure: On signal, X_1 sprints around the cone and to the line, where he shoots a ball placed on the line by X_2. X_1 continues sprinting and shooting for forty-five seconds. X_3 retrieves the balls and passes them to X_2. X_1 should not have to wait for a ball to shoot, and if one is not ready on the line, he should again sprint around the cone.
Rotate positions after forty-five seconds.
The player scoring the most goals in forty-five seconds wins.

Variation: • To emphasize conditioning, record the number of shots taken within the time period.

127

STEAL THE BACON

OFFENSIVE AND DEFENSIVE TECHNIQUES	10 Players 2 Goalkeepers	5 Balls 2 Goals

Penalty Area

Contributor: *William Muse, Princeton University, Princeton, New Jersey 08540*

Formation: The penalty area, or similar size area, can be used as a field with two portable goals. There are two teams of equal numbers. Each team stands off the field by its goal. The players on each team are assigned corresponding numbers. A goalkeeper is in each goal. A feeder, with a supply of balls, stands at the side of mid-field.

F — Feeder
G — Goalkeeper
X — Field Player
Pass – – – >
Run ——>
Ball •

Procedure: The feeder plays a ball into the middle of the field and calls a number. The player with the assigned number from each team runs to the center. The player who gains possession of the ball attacks the opposing goal and the other player defends. A one vs. one situation continues until a goal is scored or the ball goes out of bounds. When this happens, the feeder plays another ball into the middle and calls a new number.

The game can continue for a specified period of time or until one team gets a specified number of goals.

Variation:
- More than one number can be called to create two vs. two, three vs. three, etc., situations.
- Play one or two touch.
- A shot on goal must be taken before the ball is touched three times.

128

STEAL THE BACON AND COME BACK

OFFENSIVE AND   Penalty Area   12 or more Players   1 Ball
DEFENSIVE
TECHNIQUES

Formation: Six players line up along the end line, and six opponents stand along the penalty area line. A ball is midway between the lines.

X—Field Player
Run ———→
Ball .

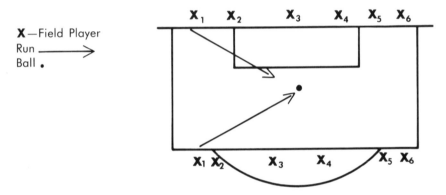

Procedure: The players on each team are given numbers corresponding to an opponent. The coach calls a number and the players with that number run to the ball. The player who reaches the ball first attempts to dribble the ball back to his line, gaining control as he reaches the line, while the opponent tries to gain possession and get it to his line.

Variation: • Call more than one number.
              • Pass to the line.

129

STOP THAT MAN

CONTAINMENT   40 yd. by 10 yd. Area   2 or more Players   3 Cones

Fitness

Formation: Two field players face each other on opposite sides of a cone which is midway between two other cones placed forty yards apart.

X—Field Player
Run
Cone

Procedure: On a signal, X_1 attempts to run and touch either of the outside cones, while X_2 attempts to prevent him by tagging him. X_1 may make feints, turns, etc. to get to a cone. Each time a cone is touched, X_1 must first return to the center cone before touching another side cone. After thirty-five seconds, the players change roles and X_2 now tries to touch the cones while X_1 contains. The player touching the most cones after one or more turns is the winner.

130

STRAIGHT SHOOTING

SHOOTING   ½ Field   1 or more Players   10 Balls
                                     1 Goalkeeper   2 Cones
                                                          Goal

Formation: A cone is placed three to four feet inside each goalpost. The shooter, with a supply of balls, is just outside the penalty area. Extra players are located behind the goal to retrieve balls and return them to extra players outside the penalty area.

G—Goalkeeper
X—Field Player
Shot ········>
Ball •
Cone ⊙

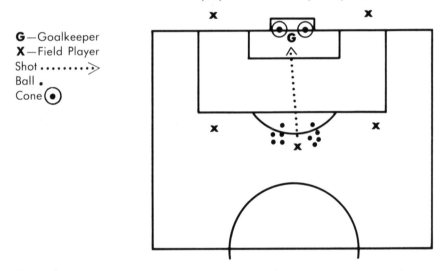

Procedure: Each player takes ten shots on goal from about twenty yards out. One point is scored for a ball that goes between the cone and goalpost.

Variation:
• Dribble full speed at goal and shoot from twenty yards away.
• Dribble full speed from the sideline and shoot when outside the penalty area.
• Add goalkeeper.
• Add defender.

131

STRIKER

SHOOTING	35 yd. by 50 yd. Area in Front of Goal	13 Players	12 Balls
		Goalkeeper	
Goalkeeping Passing			

Contributor: *Dr. Ostap Stromecky, University of Alabama, Huntsville, Alabama 35899*

Formation: Field Players form four triangles of three players each and spread out in the area outside the penalty area. One player with a supply of soccer balls is in the penalty area. A goalkeeper is in goal.

F—Feeder
G—Goalkeeper
X—Field Player
Pass — — —>
Shot ·········>
Ball •

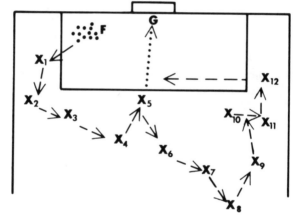

Procedure: The player in the penalty area serves as feeder and passes a ball to the number one player in the first triangle every eight seconds. The ball is passed one touch to each player within a triangle, and from triangle to triangle. The last numbered player (number twelve) in the last triangle passes the ball to the designated striker (number five), who takes a first time shot on goal.

After twelve shots, the players rotate and a new player is designated striker. This rotation continues until each player gets a chance at being striker. The player who scores the most goals becomes "The Striker."

132

TACKLE IN CONFINED AREAS

TACKLING   5 yd. by 5 yd. Area   4 to 12 Players   3 Balls

Dribbling

Formation: Four cones define a course five yards wide by ten yards long. Dribblers line up at the entrance to the course. Tacklers line up at the exit.

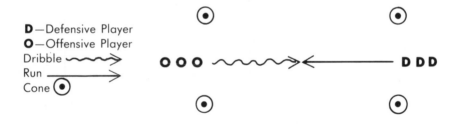

D—Defensive Player
O—Offensive Player
Dribble 〜〜〜〉
Run ⟶
Cone ⦿

Procedure: Each offensive player attempts to dribble, staying within the course, through the distant two cones. The defensive player tries to prevent the offensive player from dribbling through the course by accomplishing a legal tackle. At the conclusion of each turn, the players go to the end of the other line. The player making the most successful tackles wins.

133

TAG

| DRIBBLING | Center Circle | 6 or more Players | 2 to 4 Balls |

Formation: Two players, each with a ball, and four players without a ball, are located in the center circle.

D—Defensive Player
O—Offensive Player
Dribble 〜〜〜⟹
Ball•

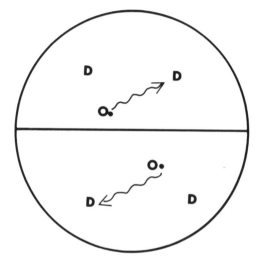

Procedure: The dribblers try to tag, with the balls, the other players who are trying to evade them. A dribbler scores one point each time he tags a player with his ball. After a pre-set time, two other players become dribblers. All players must have a chance to be dribblers. The dribbler with the most points wins.

Variation: • One more dribbler can be added for two more defenders.

134

TARGET BALL

| PASSING | Penalty Area | 14 Players | 11 Balls |

Formation: Two teams of equal numbers face each other on opposite end lines. Each team has four balls. Three target balls, a different color than the team balls, are in the center of the area. One man from each team is in the area.

X—Field Player
Pass – – – ⟩
Ball •

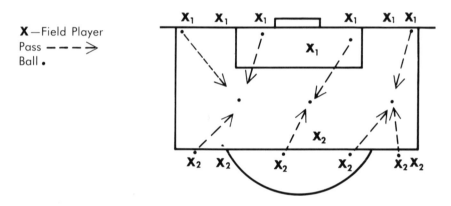

Procedure: On a signal, each team kicks their balls in an attempt to drive the target balls across the opponents' line. Each team's player in the area fields balls and returns them to his team. Players may move on either side of the area but may not cross the opposing end line. Players may not interfere with an opponent's play or kick the target balls. The first team to kick two or more target balls over the opposing line wins.

135

TEAM KEEP IT UP

JUGGLING   Any Open Area   6 or more Players   1 Ball per Group

Passing
Receiving

Formation: Players in groups of three to ten form a circle. Each group has a ball.

X—Field Player
Ball **.**

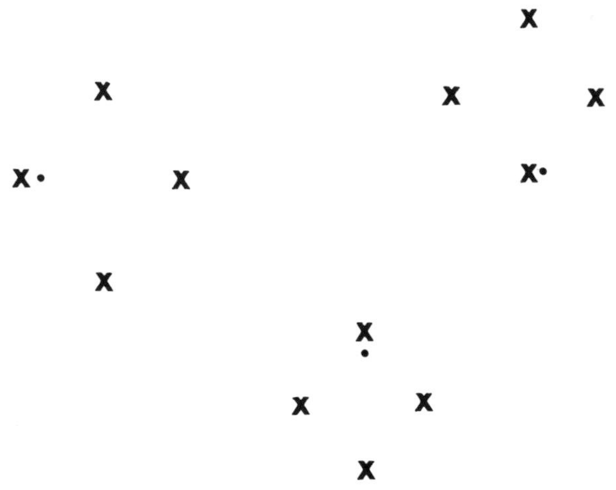

Procedure: Using soccer techniques, each group keeps the ball in the air as long as possible. The ball is passed among players in any order. A player may not juggle the ball more than three times in succession. The group completing the greatest number of touches in a designated time period wins.

136

TEAM SHOOTOUT

SHOOTING	⅓ Field	4 to 30 Players	12 Balls
		Goalkeeper	Goal

Contributor: *Fred Schmalz, University of Evansville, Evansville, Indiana 47702*

Formation: A group of offensive players, each with a soccer ball, line up about thirty-five yards from goal. An equal number of defensive players are behind the goal line. A goalkeeper is in goal.

D—Defensive Player
G—Goalkeeper
O—Offensive Player
Dribble 〜〜〜〜〉
Shot ·············〉
Ball •

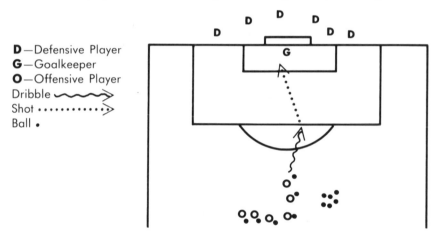

Procedure: The offensive players have three minutes to score as many points as they can by taking shootouts on goal. The players, one at a time, dribble and shoot on goal from outside the eighteen yard line. As soon as a shot is taken, the next player starts his attempt on goal. After three minutes, the groups change roles.
The offensive team earns two points for each goal, and one point for each goal save or each time the ball hits a goal post. The defensive team earns one point for each ball it clears back over the goal line while still in the air. The team scoring the most points wins.

137

TEE OFF SOCCER

KICKING   Full Field   2 or more Players   1 Ball per Player

2 Goals

Formation: Two or more players start at one goal line. Each player has a ball.

X—Field Player
Ball

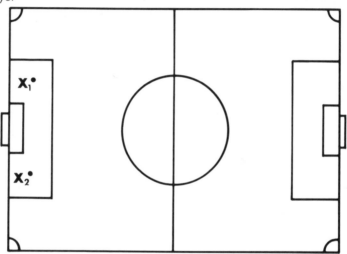

Procedure: Each player, at the same time, kicks the ball as far as he can towards the opposite goal. The purpose of the game is to score in the far goal, and again in the original goal, in as few kicks as possible. If you miss the goal and the ball goes over the end line, you must kick the ball back in front of the goal before you can score.

138

TENNIS BALL SOCCER

FITNESS	½ Basketball Court	6 to 16 Players	1 Tennis Ball
Dribbling			2 Cones

Contributor: *James W. Egli, Slippery Rock State College, Slippery Rock, Pennsylvania 16057*

Formation: Two teams (X_1 and X_2) of three players each are located within one half of a basketball court. One cone is used for each goal. The goals are placed on opposite sidelines midway between the endline and midcourt.

X—Field Player
Ball.
Cone ⊙

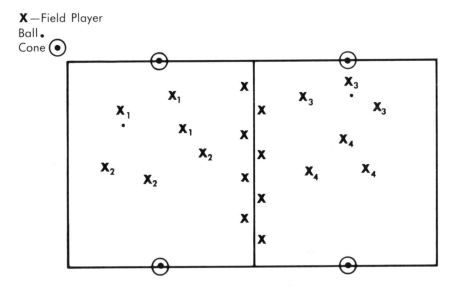

Procedure: The teams play three vs. three indoor soccer using a tennis ball. A goal is scored when the ball hits the appropriate cone. The game is played for three minutes, or until a specified number of goals are scored.

With a large group of players, a second game can be played in the other half-court. Extra players, alternating the direction they face, stand along the mid-court line and serve as a wall.

139

THE EQUALIZER

OFFENSIVE AND DEFENSIVE TECHNIQUES	40 yd. by 30 yd. Area	10 Players	1 Ball
			2 Small Goals

Formation: There are two teams of five players each in the area. One team has the ball. There are two indoor size goals, one on each end-line.

X—Field Player
Ball•

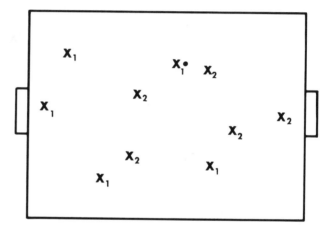

Procedure: Five players attempt to score on five other players. However, as soon as the first goal is scored, the goal into which they scored is now sealed until the other side scores. The game is over if one team scores one and prevents the other team from scoring for a set time period.

Variation: • Use regulation field with full teams.

140

THREE LEGGED SOCCER

FITNESS   Gymnasium   20 or more Players 1 Ball

Strips of Cloth

2 Indoor Goals

Formation: There are two teams of equal numbers, each team starting off in their half court area. Each player is strapped to a partner (team-mate) by wide strips of cloth at the ankle and thighs of their inside legs, thus forming three legs. There are two indoor goals and two players on each team are goalkeepers.

G—Goalkeeper
X—Field Player
Ball •

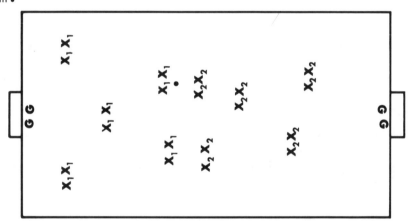

Procedure: The game is played as in regulation indoor soccer except that the players must move and play the ball with their strapped teammate.
The team ahead after a set time period wins.

141

THROW-HEAD-CATCH

HEADING	25 yd. by 25 yd. Area	8 to 22 Players	1 Ball
Fitness			2 Goals

Contributor: *Ronald W. Shewcraft, North Adams State College, North Adams, Massachusetts 01247*

Formation: Four players, X_1, play against four others, X_2, in a small field.

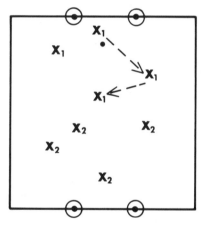

Procedure: The team in possession of the ball attempts to score in the other team's goal. A goal may only be scored by an offensive player heading the ball into the goal. The ball is in play as long as it follows a throw-head-catch sequence. A player may catch the ball with his hands only if the ball has been headed by another player (offensive or defensive). He can run with the ball in his possession and throw it to a teammate. A player receiving a thrown ball may only head the ball in order to play it to a teammate or to score a goal. A player may not throw the ball and head it to himself. The ball may be played with the head an unlimited number of times consecutively.

Variation:
- Change size of field area or goal.
- Change number of players.
- Limit number of steps taken when ball is in a player's hands.

142

THROW-IN SOCCER

THROWING   ½ Field   14 Players   1 Ball
                                        Goalkeeper

Formation: Seven attackers face seven defenders and a goalkeeper. The players are located in half-field. One of the attackers is just outside a touch line at mid-field.

D—Defensive Player
G—Goalkeeper
O—Offensive Player
Ball **.**

Procedure: The game begins with a throw-in from a touch line at mid-field. Each team gets five consecutive throw-ins followed by twenty seconds of field play after each throw. The game is stopped after twenty seconds for the next throw to be taken from the touchline nearest the point of stoppage.

Points are scored as follows:

- One point for each three or more consecutive passes from a throw-in.
- One point if a team holds the ball in play for the full twenty seconds without the opposing team touching it.
- One point for a shot on goal requiring a save by the keeper.
- Five points for a goal.

143

TOUCH THE COACH

FITNESS	10-yd. Area	2 or more Players

Contributor: *Chris Tyson, State University of New York at Stony Brook, Stony Brook, New York 11794*

Formation: Players line up in pairs, ten yards from the coach.

C —Coach
X —Field Player
Sprint ———⟹

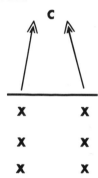

Procedure: On a whistle, the first two players race to be first to touch the coach's hand. They then go to the end of their line and the next pair starts. After each pair has gone ten times, elimination races are held. The player who gets to the coach first is the winner and sits out while the loser goes to the end of his line. Eventually only two players remain, and finally the loser.

Variation:
- The players start the race in the following positions:
  a. on their knees
  b. on their stomachs
  c. on their backs
  d. in push-up position
  e. on one leg
  f. others

- The players must perform the following activities before racing:
  a. push-ups
  b. sit-ups
  c. jump heading
  d. others

144 – TURN AND SHOOT

SHOOTING	Penalty Area	10 Players	10 Balls
Defensive Techniques,		Goalkeeper	Goal
Fitness, Goalkeeping			

Formation: A feeder stands about twenty yards from the goal. An offensive player stands near the penalty spot. A defensive player marks the offensive player. A goalkeeper is in goal. Waiting defensive players serve as retrievers behind the goal. Waiting offensive players help the feeder by supplying balls.

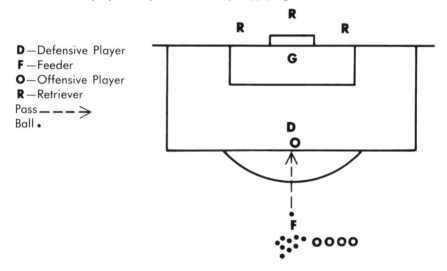

D—Defensive Player
F—Feeder
O—Offensive Player
R—Retriever
Pass _ _ _ →
Ball •

Procedure: The feeder serves a ball to the offensive player, who shoots on goal as soon as possible. After the shot is taken, the feeder serves another ball. The offensive player is under constant pressure provided by the defensive player. Each offensive player receives balls continuously for one minute. The offensive player scoring the most goals in one minute is the winner.

Variation:
  • Offensive player receives balls for one minute or until a goal is scored.
  • Increase time to one-and-one-half or two minutes.
  • Two offensive players are used. The player receiving the ball from the feeder passes, first time, to his teammate who plays on goal.

145

TWO TOUCH—ERROR EXPELS

PASSING	Full Field	22 Players	3 Balls
		2 Goalkeepers	

Formation: Players, in scrimmage vests, line up in game formation, i.e., eleven vs. eleven. Each team has at least one substitute.

G—Goalkeeper
X—Field Player
Ball●

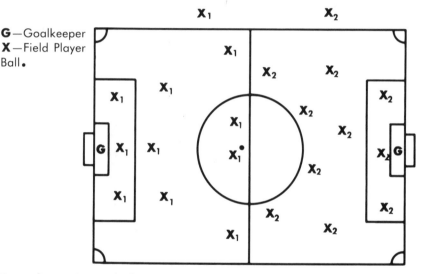

Procedure: A game of soccer is played with one restriction—the ball may only be touched two times in succession by any one player (goalkeepers are exempt from this restriction). If a player touches the ball three times in succession, he is expelled and is immediately replaced by the substitute.

Variation:
- Field players may not touch ball twice in succession, i.e., one touch soccer.
- Forwards may be allowed more touches if the play ends with a shot on goal.
- Less than eleven-man sides may be used, e.g., six vs. six, seven vs. seven, eight vs. eight.

146

TWO-TOUCH SHOOTING

SHOOTING   Full Field   14 or more Players   1 Ball

Control   2 Goalkeepers
Passing

Formation: Two teams of equal numbers are within their respective half field. A goalkeeper is in each goal. A ball is at midfield.

G—Goalkeeper
X—Field Player
Ball **.**

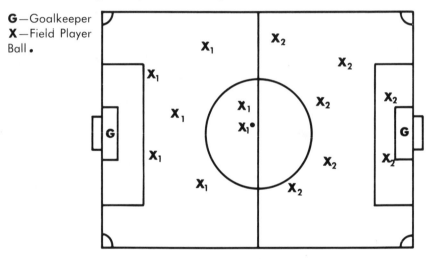

Procedure: The teams play regulation soccer with a one-touch restriction except on a shot on goal. A shot may be taken with one touch, but the only time a player is permitted a second touch is for a shot on goal. Violating this restriction results in a free kick. The team ahead after a set time wins.

147

TWO vs ONE AND GOALKEEPER

OFFENSIVE AND DEFENSIVE TECHNIQUES Goalkeeping	10 yd. by 10 yd. Area	4 Players	1 Ball
			4 Cones

Formation: Two goals are defined with cones ten yards apart. Goals are of regulation width. Two players, X_1, play against one player, X_2, and a goalkeeper, X_2.

X—Field Player
Ball.
Cone ⦿

Procedure: Two players (X_1) are on offense against one player and a goalkeeper (X_2). When X_2 gains possession, the goalkeeper becomes a field player, and one of the X_1 players drops back to become a goalkeeper. The team scoring the greater number of goals in a designated time period wins.

148

TWO vs TWO COMMUNICATION

COMMUNICATION	10 yd. by 20 yd. Area 6 Players	1 Ball
Offensive and		
Defensive Techniques		8 Cones
Passing		

Contributor: *Loren Kline, University of Delaware, Newark, Delaware 19711*

Formation: Two offensive and two defensive players are within a small field. One feeder stands within each goal of two cones.

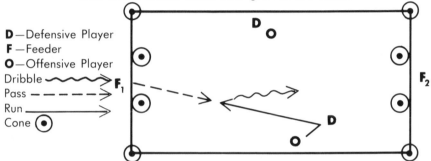

D—Defensive Player
F—Feeder
O—Offensive Player
Dribble
Pass
Run
Cone

Procedure: One of the feeders passes to an open offensive player. As the feeder passes, he calls "man on" if the intended receiver is tightly marked. In this situation, the offensive player can pass back to the feeder. If the offensive player has room, the feeder calls "hold," "turn" or "through," depending on the situation. On any of these three calls, the feeder moves into the field to create a three-on-two situation as his team attacks the small goal at the opposite end of the field. If the defense wins the ball, they counterattack. The feeder on the team that is defending may function as a goalkeeper, but is limited to the use of his feet in defending his goal. During counterattacks, the feeder becomes a supporting field player. If a goal is scored or the ball crosses the end line, the defending feeder starts the play from his end. Offensive and defensive roles now change. The team scoring the most goals in a set time wins.

Variation: • Play one vs. one, plus feeder in a smaller area.
• Build up to three vs. three or four vs. four in a larger area.

149

TWO vs TWO MOVE UP

OFFENSIVE AND DEFENSIVE TECHNIQUES	Four 10 yd. by 10 yd. Areas	16 Players	4 Balls
			32 Cones

Formation: The four areas are designated 1, 2, 3, and 4 and have cones as boundaries. A two-yard-wide goal marked by cones is at the end of each area. Two teams of two players each are in each area.

X—Field Player
Ball **.**
Cone ⊙

Procedure: Two vs. two games are played in each area. Games are of five minute duration. Games ending in ties continue until one team scores. When all games are finished, the winners move up one field while the losers move down one. (Winners in area four stay, as do losers in area one.) After three games, the two teams with the best records should be in area number four. The fourth game is the championship.

150

TWO vs TWO PRESSURE

SHOOTING	Penalty Area	4 Players	8 Balls
Receiving		2 Goalkeepers	2 Goals

Contributor: *Thomas Griffith, Dartmouth College, Hanover, New Hampshire 03755*

Formation: Two players, X_1 and X_2, compete against two others, X_3 and X_4, in the penalty area with two full-size goals and two goalkeepers. A portable goal or two sticks can be used for the second goal. A feeder, with a supply of balls, is located outside the penalty area. Players not competing serve as retrievers for the feeder.

F —Feeder
G —Goalkeeper
R —Retriever
X —Field Player
Ball .

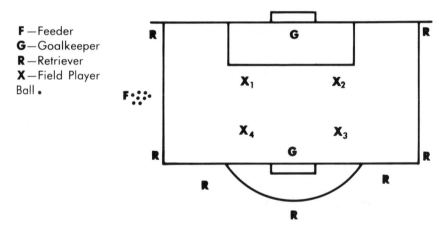

Procedure: Each pair tries to score in the appropriate goal. This is a pressure game, and balls are fed constantly, giving the players no rest for three to five minutes. The balls should be fed to force various types of shots. Goal saves are rolled to a teammate and play continues. A new ball is fed in as soon as a goal is scored or a ball goes out of bounds. The pair scoring the most goals in a set time is the winner.

Variation: • Feed ground balls.
  • Feed air balls.
  • Feed hard-driven balls.
  • Feed a variety of balls.

151

TWO vs TWO TOURNAMENT

OFFENSIVE AND DEFENSIVE TECHNIQUES	Four 10 yd. by 15 yd. Areas	16 Players	4 Balls
			24 Cones

Formation: Four ten-yard-wide by fifteen-yard-long fields are set up with cones defining boundaries. A single cone serves as a goal at the end of each miniature field. Eight two-man teams are designated. Two teams are assigned to each field to begin play.

X—Field Player
Ball .
Cone ⊙

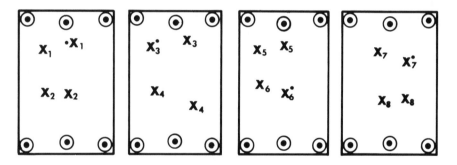

Procedure: Two vs. two games are played on each field for four minutes. The game is followed by a one-minute rest period. After the rest period each team plays a different opponent. The procedure continues until all teams have played each other. The team with the best won-loss percentage wins. If two teams are tied at the end of the round robin play, there is a playoff.

152

TWO-WAY SOCCER

PASSING	40 yd. by 40 yd. Area	8 to 10 Players	1 Ball
Goalkeeping			
Shooting		Goalkeepers	6 Cones

Contributor: Howard Goldman, Marist College, Poughkeepsie, New York 12601

Formation: Two teams of equal numbers, wearing different-colored scrimmage vests, are within the area. A cone is at each corner of the area. Two cones, fifteen to twenty feet apart, are used to define a goal in the center of the area. A goalkeeper, with a ball, is in goal.

G—Goalkeeper
X—Field Player
Ball •
Cone ⊙

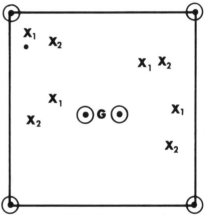

Procedure: The goalkeeper starts the game and restarts play after each goal by distributing the ball to a corner of the area. The team in possession of the ball attempts to score through either side of the goal. The goalkeeper is not on either team. Play is continuous until one team scores ten goals. Goalkeepers should be changed periodically.

Variation:
- Play one or two touch.
- Goals count only when shots are below waist.
- Goals count only when shots are on ground.
- Reduce the area and play three vs. three.

153

UP IN THE AIR

CONTROL   20 yd. by 10 yd. Area   6 Players   1 Ball

Heading
Kicking

Formation: Four players, one with a ball, spread out within the area. Defensive players must stay on the center line in the middle of the area.

D—Defensive Player
O—Offensive Player
Ball ∎

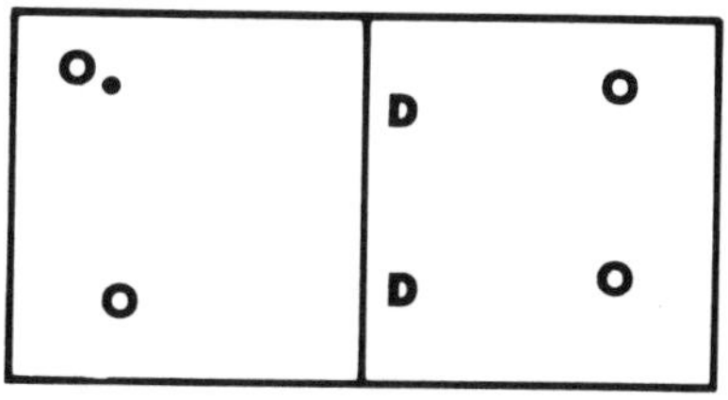

Procedure: The four players keep the ball away from the two players who must remain at all times on the center line. The ball must be kept in the air at all times. The two defenders attempt to intercept the ball and, if successful, change places with last two players to touch the ball. If a player kicks the ball out of the area, he changes places with a center-line player. The four players count the number of consecutive passes, and each new group of four attempts to beat this.

154

USE YOUR SUPPORT

SUPPORT   40 yd. by 30 yd. Area   12 Players   1 Ball
Passing

Formation: Two teams of three players each are in the area. One of the players has a ball. Six other players station themselves at the corners and mid-points of the area.

S—Support Player
X—Field Player
Ball •

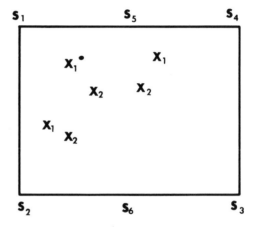

Procedure: This is a three vs. three game, with the team in possession of the ball allowed to use the perimeter players for support. S_5 and S_6 can only play the ball one touch. The corner players may also receive support passes; however, the corner player receiving the ball must pass the ball to the opposite corner (e.g., S_1 to S_2). The receiving corner man must pass the ball one touch to one of the three men in the area. After five minutes, the support players change with the field players. The team making the most one-two passes wins.

155

VOLLEY SOCCER

CONTROL	½ Field	10 to 14 Players	1 Ball
Heading			
Passing		2 Goalkeepers	
Shooting			

Formation: Two teams of equal numbers oppose each other in one half of the field. Two regulation-size goals are used, one at the end line and the other at midfield. A goalkeeper is in each goal.

G—Goalkeeper
X—Field Player
Ball

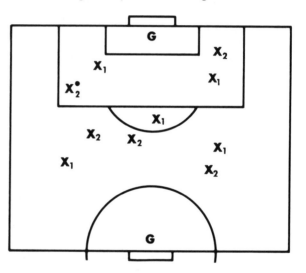

Procedure: A regulation game is played, except that the team in possession of the ball can only allow it to touch the ground twice or the other team gets the ball. The first team to score a set number of goals, or whoever is ahead after a set time period, wins.

156

WALL PASS GAME

PASSING	Center Circle	4 Players	1 Ball
			4 Cones

Formation: Use the center circle, or other similar-size area, for a small field. Make two goals about a yard wide opposite each other on the edge of the circle. Play two vs. two games within the area.

D—Defensive Player
O—Offensive Player
Pass — — — >
Run ————>
Shot •••••••>
Ball •
Cone ⊙

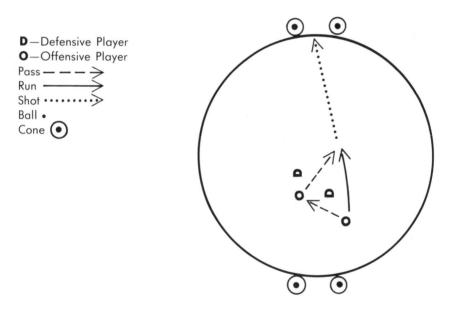

Procedure: The only way to score is directly from a wall pass maneuver with the player who receives the return pass shooting.

157

WEAVE RELAY

DRIBBLING Any Area 12 or more Players 1 Ball per Player
Fitness

Contributor: *Robert Crandall, Elmira College, Elmira, New York 14905*

Formation: Two lines are formed about ten yards apart. The players in each line are five yards apart from each other. Each player has a ball. A finish line is fifty yards away from the last player in line.

X—Field Player
Dribble ⌇⟶
Ball •

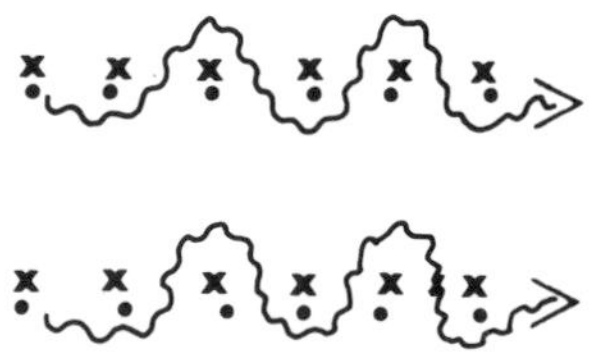

Procedure: On a signal, the first player in each line (farthest from the finish line) dribbles in figure-eight fashion around each player in his line and stops five yards from the last player. Each player dribbles in the same manner, starting as soon as the preceding player passes the player in front. This continues until all players cross the finish line. The first team to do so wins.

158

WIDE LEG ONE vs ONE

OFFENSIVE AND 10 yd. long Area   4 Players   1 Ball
DEFENSIVE
TECHNIQUES

Contributor: *Stephen Smith, Fairport Central Schools, Fairport, New York 11450*

Formation: Two players stand, with legs apart, facing each other ten yards apart. Two other players, with a ball, are midway between these players.

X—Field Player
Ball •

$$X_1 \qquad X_1 \cdot X_2 \qquad X_2$$

Procedure: X_1 and X_2 in the center play one vs. one and attempt to score a goal by passing the ball through the legs of the opposing player serving as a goal. Play continues for one minute. At the end of one minute, the players serving as goals exchange places with the central players. The two new central players now play one vs. one for one minute. The first team to score ten goals wins.

Variation: • The ball may be passed back to the teammate serving as goal who may help to beat the opponent.
• Eight players may compete instead of four. The game becomes two vs. two and the four resting players position themselves to form two goals.

159

WIN POSSESSION

MOVEMENT WITHOUT THE BALL	½ Field	11 Players	1 Ball
			Vests
Marking	Passing		

Formation: Two groups of players (X₁ and X₂) form pairs ten yards away from a player who serves as feeder. To begin, one team is designated to be on the same team as the feeding player.

F —Feeder
X —Field Player
Pass – – – >
Run ——————>
Ball •

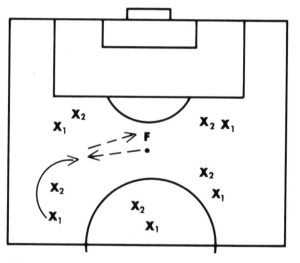

Procedure: To start, X₁ players are on the same team as the feeder. All of the players on the feeder's team attempt to free themselves. The feeder passes to one of the players on his team. This player returns the ball to the feeder. In the meantime, other X₁ players are attempting to free themselves for a return pass. The feeder and X₁ players attempt to complete as many passes in succession as possible. Each time a field player receives a pass, he must return the ball to the unmarked feeder. If an X₂ player intercepts the ball, the feeder joins that team, and X₂ players attempt to complete as many passes as possible. The team completing the most consecutive passes between themselves and the feeder wins.

160

WORLD CUP ELIMINATION

DRIBBLING	30 yd. by 30 yd. Area	4 to 6 Players	1 Ball
Shooting		Goalkeeper	1 Goal

Contributor: *Gary Parsons, Oakland College, Rochester, Michigan 48063*

Formation: Four to six field players occupy an area in front of a goal. One player has a soccer ball.

G—Goalkeeper
O—Offensive Player
X—Field Player
Ball.

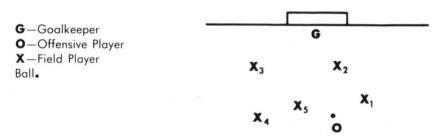

Procedure: Each player represents a different country and competes against the other players. The player with the ball attempts to score, while the other players try to prevent the score. As soon as a player scores, he sits out while the other players continue playing. When only one player is left without scoring, he is eliminated and the next round begins. Successive rounds are played until there are two players left who have not been eliminated. These two players play a one vs. one World Cup Final.